JA
V1

JAGUAR V12
Race Cars

OSPREY

Ian Bamsey
& Joe Saward

OSPREY

First published in 1986 by Osprey Publishing
Limited 12-14 Long Acre, London WC2E 9LP.
Member company of the George Philip Group

British Library Cataloguing in Publication Data

Bamsey, Ian
    Jaguar V12s.
    1.Jaguar V12 automobile-History
    I.Title
    629.2'222 TL215.J3

ISBN 0-85045-680-0

Produced by Graffiti Advertising,
Watercombe Studios, Watercombe Park, Yeovil,
Somerset BA20 2HL.

Printed in England

Sole distributors for the USA

Osceola, Wisconsin 54020, USA

JAGUAR V12

Contents

JAGUAR V12

Preface

Mosport Park has a special place in Jaguar racing lore. In the summer of 1976 Bob Tullius began a long successful association with Jaguar in professional racing at the picturesque Canadian circuit. His XJ-S finished fourth in Trans Am Category One, hampered by an overheating problem that had a straightforward solution. His team knew it had the potential to win. Sure enough, the following year Tullius took five victories and beat four race winning Porsches to the Category One title.

Nine years on Tom Walkinshaw began a World Endurance Championship bid for Jaguar at Mosport Park. At the time of writing it is too early to tell how he will fare against the dominant Group C Porsches, but the same encouraging signs were present. Walkinshaw would appear to have a sporting chance of knocking the German marque off its World Championship throne.

Jaguar and Porsche are rivals on and off the track. Each sells high performance road cars that have strong sporting overtones. Nevertheless, apart from the efforts of Tullius in American road racing and an ill fated Broadspeed European Touring Car Championship project, Jaguar neglected a strong sporting presence in the Seventies. It was a difficult decade for car manufacturers but one from which Porsche, which did continue to develop its racing heritage, emerged in the peak of fitness.

Mosport Park nine years on: the debut race for the TWR Group C Jaguar prototype. For 10 glorious laps Martin Brundle kept the car ahead of the works turbo Porsches, then a combination of cockpit boost control and a tightening wheel bearing left the Rothmans cars in the lead. However, Brundle and partner Thackwell switched to join Schlesser in the second car (No. 52) and, delayed by a mysterious vibration, it came home in a worthy third place.

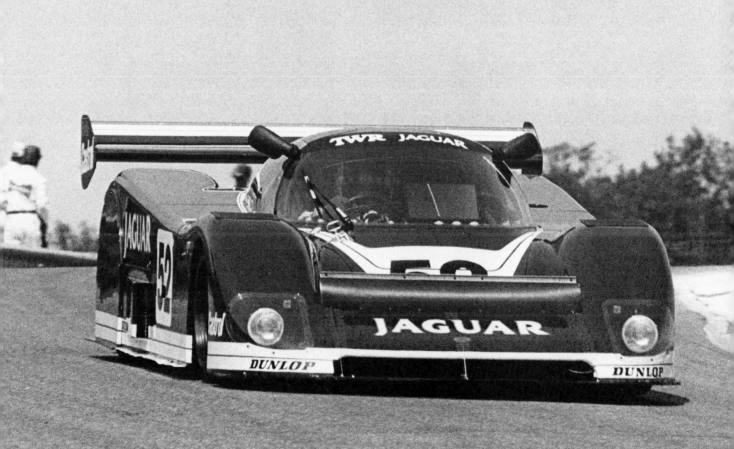

Since Jaguar won back its independence in 1980 it has undertaken an increasingly ambitious racing programme. In 1984 Tullius took the marque back to Le Mans. Respecting its heritage and improving its image: those are two of the company's key objectives. Porsche owes much of its mystique to a long history of competition success and has never been known to rest on its laurels.

One can often justify racing to an accountant in terms of publicity - especially TV exposure - but it is image rather than awareness where the real return is. The customer knows the brand names and reputations. How he or she perceives the product is what counts. That is where racing can be more powerful than advertising. Today Jaguar recognises that the battle on the track is a vital ingredient in the battle in the showroom. This book is a tribute to those fighting that battle on its behalf in the Eighties.

Pit stop for Jaguar's smart TWR prototype - en route for a fine finish in its first race.

JAGUAR V12

Acknowledgements

Special thanks are due to Bob Tullius and the Group 44 team, in particular Lawton Foushee, to Tom Walkinshaw and his crew and to Andy Rouse. Their kind co-operation made this book possible. The authors are also grateful to Jaguar personnel Colin Cook and Ian Norris (UK) and Mike Cook (USA) for providing valuable additional assistance.

The photographs come from a variety of sources, but in particular we are indebted to the picture libraries of Jaguar Cars Inc., Bob and Lisa Newsome, John Overton and Chris Harvey.

Kick off for Bob Tullius (right, upper photograph) and Tom Walkinshaw. Tullius' Jaguar association began in 1974 with this British Leyland Inc. backed E type, while Walkinshaw's involvement with the marque did not start until the Eighties and it was not until 1983 that he received official blessing for his XJ-S ETCC campaign.

JAGUAR V12

Project V12

Jaguar withdrew its factory racing team following the great C and D type years of 1951-56. The company considered a replacement for the '55 and '56 Le Mans winning car to be essential if it was to keep on top of the opposition, but didn't have the resources to commit to such a development. Nevertheless, it continued to support private entries and was rewarded with a third D type Le Mans win in 1957, before a 3.0 litre capacity restriction finally pushed the D type out of the forefront of international sportscar racing.

With the demise of the D type, Jaguar's main concern became production based competition and in 1962 this enforced policy took on a new significance as the sportscar World Championship was switched to production based GT cars. Jaguar still didn't have the resources to support a full works team but the Browns Lane competition department's E types were campaigned by a number of competitive private teams in selected events, including Le Mans.

Sadly the E type years at Le Mans ('62-'64) brought less success than might have been hoped for, and in any event the classic French race continued to run prototypes so the World Championship contenders were somewhat overshadowed. 1962 marked the last win for a front engined sports-racing car at Le Mans, a Ferrari Testa Rossa heading the GT cars home. 1963 ushered in a new era of mid engine prototypes, a Ferrari 250P leading the way.

The early Sixties were Ferrari days at La Sarthe, but in 1964 Ford joined in the game with the promising new GT40. 1965 promised a great deal as Ford would put the lessons of its first prototype racing season into practice and Jaguar was poised to re-enter the fray ....

Although it had concentrated on customer support for eight years, the factory competition department had been kept in a state of constant readiness for a works racing return. The marque held racing high on its list of priorities. It knew that the glorious years at Le Mans had done wonders for its prestige. Lofty England, who masterminded the works victories, recalled that when he first visited the States in 1948, "people didn't even know what a Jaguar car was ... but as soon as we won Le Mans people who were interested in cars ... knew what a Jaguar was and the name went forward very quickly".

The company had begun design work on a 5.0 litre racing engine, to replace the D type's 3.8 litre converted road unit, in the mid Fifties, but the 3.0 litre sportscar formula rendered it obsolete. It was not until the mid Sixties that the Claude Baily design was once again eligible for World Championship sportscar racing. Baily's V12 was significant in that although a no-compromise racing engine, it was the sort of engine that Jaguar wanted in a future road car range.

15

The lithe lines of Jaguar's XJ13 Le Mans car contrast
strongly with those of the contemporary XJ saloon. The
mid Sixties prototype was streamlined in classical race car
tradition but did not harness the wind to provide
downforce. It was born at a time when the potential of
aerodynamic downthrust was just beginning to be under-
stood, and its race programme was cancelled before its
shape could be put to the acid test...

The V12 engine took a low priority after
1958 - it became little more than a design study
until, in 1964, the factory once more embarked
on a quest for Le Mans glory. By the end of that
year the design had been translated into metal
and was running on the test bed.

While Baily at last saw his baby born,
engineering director William Heynes appointed
chassis specialist Derek White to produce a
suitable prototype, with aerodynamics by the
company's long standing specialist Malcolm
Sayer.

A former aircraft engineer, Sayer designed
the functional, streamlined D type which proved
so effective at cheating the wind on Le Mans'
three mile long Mulsanne straight, and subse-

quently dictated the shape of the road going E
type, the lines of which were so clearly related to
those of its illustrious racing predecessor. Over
the '62-'64 seasons he was responsible for the
aerodynamics of a number of 'low drag' racing E
types.

Sayer worked mathematically to derive his
basic design, later testing the result by putting a
scale model in the Royal Aircraft Establishment,
Farnborough's wind tunnel. A truly brilliant
man by all accounts, the XJ (Experimental
Jaguar) 13, as the new prototype was to be called, was his first mid engine racing design. The
shape he produced, mid engine layout notwithstanding, was very much of the D and E
type school. It was curvaceous and undoubtedly
very slippery, but paid little, if any, heed to the
role of aerodynamic downforce in racing car performance.

Sayer was in good company. Porsche did not
come to fully appreciate the importance of
downforce in the design of racing prototypes until JW Automotive put a higher drag, higher

downforce tail onto its 917 in late 1969 and in so doing transformed an unwieldy machine into a quicker, more stable proposition.

In comparison with the shape of the pace setters of 1965, the Ford GT40 and Ferrari P2, the XJ13 appears innocently streamlined and uncluttered, devoid even of a rear spoiler. It is clear that Sayer had not read the messages sent out by the far sighted Eric Broadley in the form of his 1963 Lola GT and 1964 Ford GT40 designs, which set the pattern for the future of prototypes, right up until the coming of ground effect technology in the late Seventies. Having split with Ford early in 1964, Broadley penned his classic Lola T70 from which his Nimrod-Aston Martin of the 1980s was a clear derivative.

The XJ13 was designed at the same time as the T70; on the face of it its D type roots were anchoring it in a quickly passing racing era. A sudden reversal of racing policy early in 1965 means that it never took the acid test.

In some respects the XJ13 design was in the vanguard of contemporary racing technology, under the skin. White, an ex-Connaught man, opted for a monocoque chassis plus fully stressed drivetrain. However, the front body section of the car was an integral part of the structure, whereas the modern trend (as typified by the T70) was for a completely separate GRP bodyshell, the shape of which could be easily changed, and which was lighter, and less costly to repair in the event of a shunt.

The XJ13's 18 gauge aluminium alloy sheet monocoque incorporated wide sills which ran down either side from the stressed front bulkhead and were joined towards the rear by a triangular box section which ran transversally, behind the driver, forming the rear cockpit bulkhead. A total of 40 gallons was contained in Marston rubber fuel cells housed in the sills and transverse box section. The sills ran beyond the rear bulkhead to partially enclose the V12 engine, which was attached to them via a tubular structure either side, and was also bracketed to the rear bulkhead.

The rear suspension was hung from the back of the drivetrain and incorporated fabricated lower wishbones and twin parallel radius arms

but, in another departure from common contemporary practice, used the driveshafts in place of upper wishbones. At the front was a pair of fabricated wishbones. It was Heynes who wanted to use this adapted E type suspension and he got his way when White left following the cancellation of the racing programme. The springing medium was conventional; Armstrong supplied spring-damper units, one at each corner, and there was a front and rear anti-roll bar.

The XJ13's ventilated disc brakes were mounted outboard and were switched from the traditional Dunlop to the more common Girling racing units. However, Dunlop supplied the 15in. cast magnesium wheels and tyres.
ZF supplied the 5 speed racing gearbox, as used in the GT40, and a twin plate clutch transmitted the power of the 5.0 litre engine.

Baily's fuel injected, twin overhead camshafts per bank unit produced 502 bhp at 7600 rpm and the entire package weighed in at 1050 kg. By way of comparison, a 1965 4.0 litre V12 Ferrari P2 produced around 410 bhp but weighed in at less than 850 kg. The rival GT40 began its career in 4.0 litre guise, producing less than 400 bhp while weighing only 850 kg, but over the '65 and '66 seasons was increased in capacity to 7.0 litres, to produce well in excess of 500 bhp, at the same time incurring extra weight, to the extent that it ended up almost as heavy as the XJ13.

The Jaguar engine, on paper, was a potential Le Mans winner but the XJ13's chassis was heavy and in a number of respects, aside from its fully stressed drivetrain, was dated. When White left after the sudden demise of the race programme early in 1965, Mike Kimberley, a young Jaguar engineer who went on to become managing director of Lotus, was given the task of completing the build (modified E type suspension and all). This job was given low priority and was not finished until February 1966, when the beautiful beast was put under dust sheets.

Jaguar's 1966 merger with BMC made the resurrection of a racing programme less likely, but Kimberley was instructed to keep an eye on the opposition. Over the years 1965-67 Ford committed ever greater resources to its Le Mans

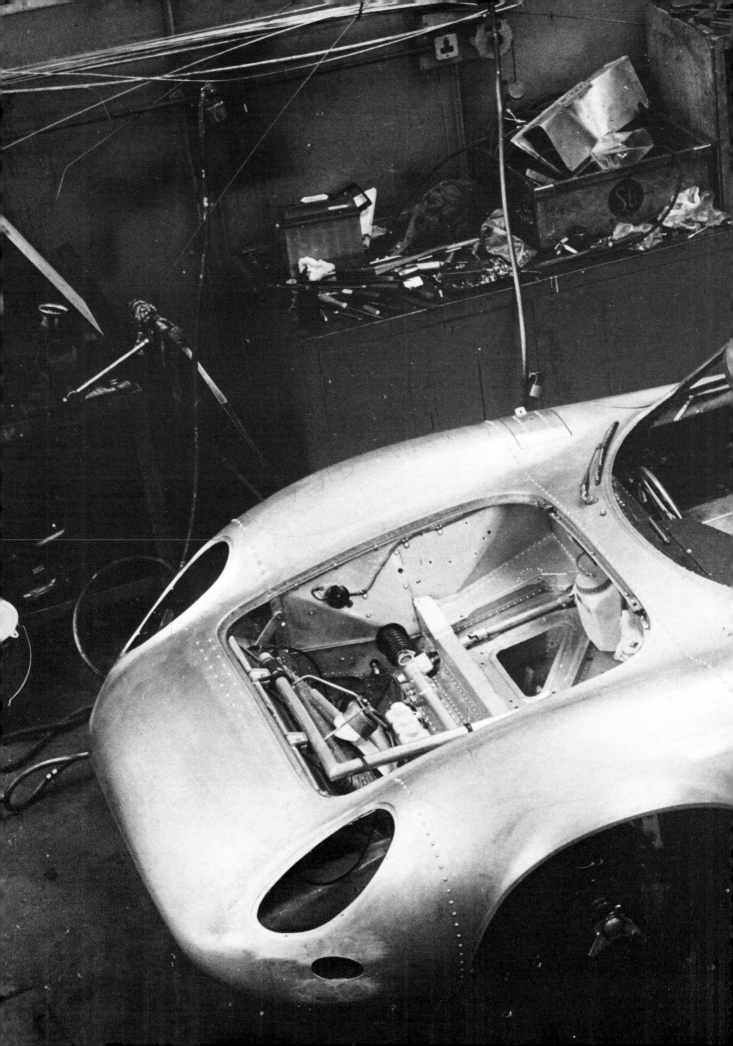

A rare photograph of the V12 engined XJ13 prototype under construction at Browns Lane in 1965. Before the car was completed the decision had been taken to abandon the Le Mans bid. Note how the nose section forms part of the monocoque: contemporary cars had detachable GRP body sections which hid all the structural elements of the car.

bid, to the extent that the American giant had 13 cars in the 1966 race, including eight 7.0 litre machines. Jaguar's change of heart had been well timed.

The XJ13 was kept a secret but in March 1967 it was quietly given a run - Norman Dewis apparently taking it to MIRA while Lofty England turned a blind eye. The story goes that Sir William Lyons eventually got to hear of it and rapped Dewis on the knuckles, at the same time asking him, with a smile, 'how did she go?'. The answer was a drama-free 161.6 mph average on the banked course, reaching 175 mph on the straights.

Ex-Daimler apprentice David Hobbs, on the verge of a long professional racing career, was at the wheel and was only sent out after the old E2A D type derivative, painted a matching dark green colour, had done a number of 'decoy' laps. Later, the XJ13 was more daringly run at Silverstone on a couple of occasions, both Hobbs and Richard Attwood doing the driving. The up-and-coming drivers were impressed with the car.

It was difficult to judge its pace, given that the circuit was not used for World Championship sportscar racing at the time, but it was a few seconds off what would have been respectable for lesser competition. Of course, it had not undergone any development over its two year existence. Which was just as well, for in the middle of 1967 a new 3.0 litre capacity limit was announced, to take effect from the start of the 1968 season ....

All was not lost. Baily's V12 did eventually form the basis of a new road engine. This was the creation of Walter Hassan, who took overall

responsibility for engine development following the retirement of Heynes in 1969. Hassan remained with the company until 1972 - just long enough to see his V12 road engine launched in the Series 3 E type.

Baily's 1955-conceived design was a 60 degree V12 with a seven main bearing aluminium block, aluminium twin overhead camshaft heads, XK style hemispherical com-

From the front the attractive XJ13 bore a strong resemblance to its D type predecessor. Both cars were of sensuous appearance: the XJ13's brasher contemporaries were arguably more functional.

bustion chambers and Lucas mechanical fuel injection. With a bore of 87 mm and a stroke of 70 mm, it displaced 4991 cc. It was safe for up to 8500 rpm. A wet sump road version developed alongside the dry sump racing unit was Hassan's starting point.

A road going version of the XJ13 prototype was a concept that had been considered but rejected. Nevertheless, V12 power was seen as a logical choice for the future flagships of the marque. The V12 option promised greater appeal in the marketplace than a V8 alternative, particularly in the USA where V8s were commonplace. A V12 engine was far more sophisticated; since the Fifties the layout had become the hallmark of Ferrari, and later Lamborghini. Jaguar spoke of "taking the magic world of 12 cylinder motoring to a far wider cross-section of automobile connoisseurs than ever before".

On a practical level, the V12 layout promised exceptional smoothness; like Jaguar's traditional straight six, the V12 is inherently free of primary or secondary out of balance forces.
A major departure from the original V12 was in Hassan's choice of single cam heads. This was largely due to a desire to keep the unit as light, compact and quiet as possible. With single cam heads the unit was able to squeeze into the same underbonnet space as required for the XK six cylinder and was cheaper to produce. The change brought no serious drawback. On the road the engine was not required to rev so highly and the single cam head allowed in line, vertical valves of adequate size for efficient breathing up to 6500 rpm. Higher engine speeds would have caused major noise supression problems.

The single cam engine was developed in conjunction with Weslake's flat head combustion chamber, Hassan considering this type of chamber the optimum for an over-square multicylinder road engine. Fairly deep bowl-in-piston chambers were tried, but more power was obtained with shallower chambers of greater diameter. Hassan then backed up his move with practical tests which showed that the single cam flat head was better in all respects than the original dohc hemi, up to 5000 rpm. Bench tests 21

Although the XJ13 didn't race, it has had a long public career as a show car (as pictured here), to the delight of many thousands of Jaguar enthusiasts. The car was not run in public before the launch of the Jaguar V12 road engine and sadly it was badly damaged just prior to that occasion during the making of a promotional film. Thankfully the original body formers had (by sheer luck) escaped destruction and Abbey Panels of Coventry was able to fully restore its original handiwork. Note the conventional boot — a most unusual appendage for a mid Sixties prototype...

showing in particular a stronger torque curve were followed by conclusive road tests, a Mk 10 saloon with the new engine being run alongside a similar model with the old wet sump unit.

Early Lucas mechanical injection, as used on the racing engine was investigated for the flat head and good power and torque figures were obtained, but exhaust emission proved a problem, given the strict US legislation brought in during the late Sixties and early Seventies. Lowering the compression ratio from 10.6:1 to 9:1 enabled 97 rather than 99 octane petrol to be used, helping to clean the exhaust, but Hassan was forced to switch to carburettors to solve the problem. He opted for a pair of Stromberg 175 CD SEs feeding each bank. The inlet ports were located inside the vee but by putting the carbs outside he kept the overall engine height down (important from the point of view of the bonnet line of front engined cars) and the consequently long inlet tracts produced a torque-improving ram effect. Suitable three-branch manifolds were water heated, at about 100 degrees centigrade. Fuel was fed to the carburettors by SU AVF 106 electric pumps at 1.5 lb/sq. in.

Naturally, the exhaust manifolding was kept on the outside of the vee, paired pipes from each bank feeding two main pipes. Hassan took the flat head out to 90 x 70 mm for a 5343 cc displacement. Despite the large capacity, thanks to its aluminium block, heads and sump it weighed little more than Jaguar's biggest, 4.2 litre, six. Power was quoted as 272 bhp at 5850 rpm, torque as 304 lb/ft at 3600 rpm.

Looking at it in detail, the 1971 released Jaguar V12 has wet liners of cast iron, as are the four bolt caps for the seven 3 in. main bearings that support the forged steel crankshaft. This three plane, Tuftrided item is balanced statically and dynamically and has a rubber/steel vibration damper. Its front seal is a lip-type, the rear of asbestos rope. Forged steel I-section con rods are paired on 2.3 in. diameter journals and have bronze bushed little ends. Each Hepworth piston has three rings.

The spark plugs are located near the centre, firing from the inlet side. The alloy heads are sand cast and have 40 degree inlet ports. Each

head is attached to the block by 26 studs. The valve guides are cast iron and the 90 degree valve seats are of sintered iron. The inlet valves are of EN52 silicon chrome steel while the exhaust valves are of 21-4 WS austenitic steel. Both ports have a diameter of 7.74 mm.

The camshafts operate the valves through chilled cast iron bucket tappets with shim adjustment. The valve lift is inlet: 418 mm; exhaust: 346 mm. Tappet clearances are 0.30 to 0.35 mm, cold. The valve timing is inlet: 17 degrees BTDC, 59 degrees ABDC; exhaust: 59 degrees BBDC, 17 degrees ATDC.

The camshafts and tappets run directly in an alloy tappet block, which has seven camshaft bearings with diecast alloy caps. The camshaft drive is a traditional roller chain; a single-stage duplex item of 9.5 mm pitch. This is tensioned by a Morse tensioner incorporating a Nylatron GS blade and anti-backlash device. It is driven by a 21 tooth camshaft sprocket. A distributor jackshaft within the vee takes advantage of the camshaft drive. It runs on white metal bearings.

With the V12 Jaguar became the first company to specify Lucas Mk2 OPUS transistorised ignition, favoured primarily for its ever-consistent timing. It dispenses with conventional contact breakers, relying instead on an electro-magnetic pick up. Developed from Formula One racing, it feeds 600 sparks per second at 6000 rpm, with a capacity of up to 700 per second. The distributor is a Lucas 36 DE12, the coil a Lucas oil-filled 13C 12. Lucas also supply the pre-engaged M45G starter, fed from a Lucas RXCA 55/8 battery as standard. The plugs are 14 mm Champion N9Ys while the altenator is a Butec A7/1A with a 60 amp capacity.

Jaguar's magnificent V12 engine was launched in 1971 as a boost for the ageing E type. The Series 3 version of the classic sportscar was given a sophisticated image (note the driver in the publicity shot!) and no official attempt was made to use it in competition for three years. However, factory engineer Peter Taylor took it upon himself to enter a pre-production model (a Series 2 uprated to Series 3 specification) for British production sportscar club racing and his virtually standard racer (lower photograph) won a national title.

Jaguar V12 Race Cars

The alternator is belt driven from the nose of the crankshaft, as is the single centrifugal impeller type water pump which feeds both banks of cylinders. The cooling system also cools the oil via a heat exchanger in the front of the long, shallow sump. The lubrication system, working at up to 70 lb/sq. in, uses a crescent type oil pump, as found in automatic transmissions.

The magnificent V12 unit was first shown in public in the suitably facelifted E type early in 1971. The engine was married either to a familiar four speed manual box or an automatic transmission and structurally the ageing sports car was essentially unchanged from its six cylinder guise. However, the bulkhead at the front of the basic monocoque and the tubular framework projecting ahead of it to carry the engine and front suspension was redesigned and strengthened. Only the longer, 8ft. 9in. (2+2) wheelbase option was offered, either in open/roadster or fixed head/coupé form.

The Series 3 E type was followed in 1972 by a similarly powered XJ saloon, the XJ12, and this was later made available in two door coupé form. However, 1975, the year when the charismatic E type was phased out, brought a true *Gran Turismo* coupé, the XJ-S. Based on familiar XJ mechanicals (with E type-style rear suspension, albeit with twin coil spring/damper units, wishbone plus coil spring/damper front suspension and discs front and rear), this strikingly styled two-plus-two came with the V12 fuel injected courtesy of a Lucas/Bosch system.

The mid Seventies saw the first serious competition work for the V12; ironically with the dying E type and albeit at an amateur racing level. The first production category E type appeared on the track in the U.K., in the hands of Jaguar development engineer Peter Taylor. His privately owned and run chassis was the first V12 built (EX100), the history of which went back to 1969. Taylor ran under RAC rules which allowed little in the way of modifications and grouped cars by U.K. retail price. He regularly won his class and took the national title.

In the USA amateur sportscar racing held far more prestige as there was less road racing vying for media and public attention and two

Series 3 E types that appeared in SCCA B Production in 1974 carried British Leyland Inc. logos. These more highly modified cars backed by the American importer were developed and run by Huffaker Engineering Inc. on the west coast and by Group 44 Inc. in the east, each team acting independently and concentrating on its own regional championship. The two teams only met for the national run-off, the single event which traditionally determines the SCCA's national titles for its amateur categories.

The officially supported American programmes were an extension of the importer's regular

First and latest versions of the Jaguar V12 engine. The current s.o.h.c. unit (left) has its origins in the d.o.h.c. four valve race engine that was intended to power the ill fated XJ13 (above). In 1981 the spin-off two valve road engine was uprated to H.E. specification by the adoption of special cylinder heads designed by the Swiss engineer Michael Mays in the interests of better fuel economy (left). The mid Eighties prototypes used a development of the original Weslake flat head in pursuit of high power levels.

involvement in SCCA racing, which for many years had embraced Triumph and MG sports cars run by specialist teams such as Huffaker and Group 44. The idea of adding the E type to the stable came from Group 44. Having accepted the idea, the importer supplied cars, parts and some funds, as usual; there was no other works involvement, and no direct communication took place between the teams and Coventry.

The American E type programme lasted until the Series 3 stocks had been exhausted in the USA: by the end of 1975 the teams had each won regional titles and Group 44 had taken the 1975 national crown. It was not until 1976 that the V12 was seen in professional racing; that year Group 44 won the importer's support for a switch to the XJ-S and a crack at the Trans Am series, making an exploratory entry at Mosport Park in Canada. It didn't win its class but the début was sufficiently encouraging for a 1977 title bid.

Less encouraging was the début, the following month, of the parent company's contender for the equivalent series in Europe, the European Touring Car Championship. Whereas British Leyland simply approved the American

SCCA E type to Le Mans prototype... between 1974 and 1984 the Jaguar V12 engine powered increasingly ambitious racing programmes on both sides of the Atlantic. Bob Tullius started the ball rolling with his B Production Series 3 E type (top left) and while he went on to tackle the SCCA's Trans Am series with an XJ-S, British Leyland embarked on a European Touring Car Championship programme with the less suitable XJ12C (below). The American programme was as successful as the European programme was unsuccessful. Although the latter fizzled out in disgrace, the marque's reputation was restored on the circuits of Europe by Tom Walkinshaw's Eighties XJ-S campaign (lower left). In 1984 Walkinshaw won the European Touring Car Championship and Tullius took his IMSA prototype to Le Mans (above), fulfilling a dream for himself and all Jaguar enthusiasts.

importer's financial-support-only for Group 44, the ETCC effort, although handled by Broadspeed, was a real factory team. Leyland Cars, as Jaguar's parent company was now calling itself, was making an ambitious attempt to improve its corporate image in the European marketplace. For marketing considerations it defied racing logic, opting for the XJ12 coupé rather than the more suitable, lighter XJ-S. And it was a Leyland rather than a Jaguar racer, the conglomerate (within which the classic marque was in danger of losing its identity) saying: "for far too long we have suffered from having a fragmented public image - the buying public rarely identifies the Leyland name with the car range we produce, and indeed at this time it does not benefit from the combined strengths of the good reputations possessed by Austin-Morris, Rover, Triumph, MG, Jaguar, and so on.

"Leyland Cars is now in every sense a unified company. We want the glamour of the Jaguar name to be reflected in all our products."

It didn't work. Neither the XJ12 racing pro-gramme nor the concept of submerging Jaguar in Leyland Cars was a success. While Group 44 was busy winning Trans Am titles in 1977 and '78, the Broadspeed programme fizzled out prematurely, in disgrace. And commercially Jaguar was running into trouble on both sides of the Atlantic. After 1978 Group 44 took a break from promoting the marque for the first time in five years.

Jaguar didn't revive until it was freed from its Leyland shackles. The escape came in 1980 and the now independently managed company's American arm immediately took a bold step, agreeing to fund the design of a Jaguar powered prototype with long term Le Mans potential for Group 44. The marque's Le Mans tradition was the deciding factor in Group 44's sales pitch to it. Now headed by John Egan, the company appreciated that its great Fifties racing heritage had helped keep it alive through the dark days of the late Seventies. As the revitalised organisation rebuilt its strength, the prototype would warm up in the American IMSA series, following a

design/build year (1981) during which Group 44 would chase yet another Trans Am title. Group 44's return to campaigning Jaguars was, the American operation admits, initially window dressing. Times were still hard.

By the time that Group 44 had come second overall in the 1981 Trans Am, Jaguar was firmly on the road to recovery, helped by rejuvenated sales in the USA. The prototype started racing in the States in 1982 and that year the parent company helped Tom Walkinshaw Racing exploit the potential of the XJ-S in the ETCC. Group 44 was in the process of becoming a factory team and in 1983 the works gave its official blessing to TWR, following a successful learning year.

The biggest step came in 1984, when Coventry gave its approval for Group 44 to fulfill its aspiration to take the marque back to Le Mans, following an encouraging period of IMSA racing. The cars didn't win the classic but they gave a good account of themselves. TWR also had Le Mans aspirations and talked the

company into supporting it in a Group C programme following a successful 1984 ETCC title bid. So by 1985 the marque had two prototype teams, one supported by its American marketing operation, the other by the equivalent 'rest of the world' operation, both enjoying full technical support from Browns Lane.

After the end of the D type programme Sir William Lyons had said "the company has not lost interest in racing. We have not neglected the necessary development work for a return to the sport. We have made certain plans but just when we put them into operation must depend on circumstances".

Between the BMC merger of 1966 and the granting of a new independence in 1980, circumstances were wrong for any sort of ambitious racing programme. Happily, the return to freedom brought a very different set of circumstances ....

Brian Redman led Klaus Ludwig's Mustang for the first 28 laps of the 1984 Miami Grand Prix. Then the Mustang got ahead - but had rooted its tyres and Redman, sharing with Doc Bundy, went on to win.

Tom Walkinshaw's Group A XJS made its British début at Donington Park in May 1982 where the Scotsman proved the car was a potential BMW beater by leading in the early stages of the race. Sadly, a stone holed the radiator costing Walkinshaw and co-driver Chuck Nicholson their chance of victory.

Walkinshaw and Nicholson came back to Donington
Park in 1983 with open factory support. Although
they again retired, a sister car driven by Fitz-
patrick/Brundle/Calderari took the honours.

In 1984 the TWR Group A/XJS
came of age, winning seven rounds
of the European Touring Car
Championship. Here Nicholson
and Win Percy sweep to a popular
win on home soil at Donington.

The much improved 1985 XJR-5 showed promising form in the early season races in Florida, but both the Group 44 entries suffered an unhealthy number of mishaps. Here at Sebring car 44 (Bob Tullius/Chip Robinson/Jim Adams) lost 20 laps due to a brush with a tyre wall and dropped to fourth place.

Car 44, driven by Tullius/Redman/Bundy, leading Le Mans in 1984 at the end of the first hour, while the Porsches refuelled.

Le Mans 1984, car 44 survived the night in a top six
position. An early morning gear failure heralded sad
retirement despite the gallant efforts of the pit crew.

Here sandwiched by the XJR-5s at Watkins Glen, the Randy Lanier/-Bill Whittington Blue Thunder March-Chevrolet won the 1984 Camel GT title. The March wasn't any faster than the Jaguars, but made good mileage out of the Porsches' long delay in getting up to speed ... while Group 44 was preoccupied with Le Mans.

Clean lines of the XJR-5 on its Daytona 24 hour début, early in 1983. Tullius/Bill Adam/Pat Bedard ran with the leaders in the early stages, before becoming delayed by a broken right front wheelbearing, which led to suspension failure.

No joy for car 04 at Daytona in 1985. Robinson/-Adams/Ballot-Lena were delayed by a blown tyre before retiring with zero oil pressure.

Heading for home. With three retirements to haunt him (both cars in '84, then his sister car during the night of the '85 race), Tullius still has a chance to get car 44 home. A dropped valve almost cost that chance, but the Group 44 chief finally saw the finish on 11 cylinders.

Pocono in 1984 was one of a series of late season events at which the Group 44 Jaguars were hard pushed to keep the Al Holbert/Derek Bell Porsche 962 in sight. This is the Tullius car.

Ready for take-off ... the 3½ mile long
Mulsanne straight beckons one of the XJR-5s to
come and top 200 mph. Both cars could achieve
such a speed, but neither was fast enough to
worry the Porsches at Le Mans in '85.

JAGUAR V12

The S.C.C.A. V12s

In 1973 British Leyland was working well in the USA and racing was working well as a means of promoting its MG and Triumph sports cars. Bob Tullius had an MGB, a Spitfire, a TR6 and a GT6 in his Group 44 team's British Leyland USA backed line up, but hankered for something a little more ambitious after years of small capacity SCCA competition. He suggested pitting the hard-to-sell V12 E type, the performance and looks of which had suffered under increasingly stringent emission and safety legislation, against the Chevrolet Corvettes in B Production.

Merle Brennan's racing E type had boosted sales of the British sportscar back in the mid '60s by winning 39 of the 42 SCCA races it contested over the period 1964-66 and racing was in the import operation's blood. British Leyland Inc. marketing chief, Mike Dale, an ex-Healey man and earnest believer in the power of racing as a promotional tool, welcomed Tullius' suggestion. If successful, it would not only help shift stock but would also be a boost for a proud marque that was fast losing its identity within the BL conglomerate, thanks to politics across the Atlantic.

Dale duly commissioned both Group 44 which moved from its original Falls Church, Virginia base to Dulles Airport near Washington in 1974, and Huffaker Engineering of San Raphael, California to begin regional B Produc-tion campaigns in 1974.

Joe Huffaker had run Brennan's E type, and other successful examples in the Sixties. Originally from Indiana, the 46 year old British sports car preparation expert had moved to California as a teenager and had quickly become involved in the local racing scene. It was in the mid Fifties that he became involved in racing full time and he built his first road racing car from the remains of an early Austin Healey. That was followed by a Chevrolet powered single seater for one Fred Knoop which proved so successful that he was invited to manage San Francisco based BMC distributor Kjell Qvale's competitions department.

While working for Qvale, Huffaker designed the remarkable "MG Liquid Suspension Special" - a competitive mid-60s Indy Car which employed MG 1100 'hydralastic' suspension. Huffaker set up on his own in the late Sixties, racing MGs and developing special road equipment for the marque. His was an importer-sponsored team, like Group 44, and with Huffaker's E type background it was a natural choice for a 1974 B Production programme.

In the east, Tullius similarly had long standing connections with British Leyland, on the Triumph rather than the MG side. Tullius had ten years road racing experience, although it had originally been his ambition to become a pro footballer. A knee injury had put paid to the 49 hopes of the New York State high school and college star. A plumber's son, he had subsequently enjoyed drag racing and motorcycle scrambling but had not been introduced to road racing until he was into his twenties.

Robert Charles Tullius was working as a Kodak rep. based in his home town of Rochester, NY when he came across an SCCA meeting at the Old Marlborough Raceway and resolved to join in the fun. He bought a used Triumph TR3 in 1961 and quickly started beating drivers of the newer TR4 model. It didn't take him long to approach Standard Triumph to ask for the sort of backing his TR4 rivals were getting, but it was a while before the importer agreed to support him. His first, formal approach having been turned down, Tullius made another trip to the company's New York offices and this time waited patiently for the president, Martin Tustin, to leave work. He intercepted

him with a characteristic, first class piece of salesmanship that resulted in the supply of a brand new powder blue TR4 in the late spring of '62.

Alas, Tullius' new car was quickly written off in avoidance of another competitor's broken-off exhaust pipe. It took more powerful persuasion to get the $500 cheque out of Standard Triumph to buy another wreck, so that he could

Joe Huffaker's E type was almost identically prepared to that of Bob Tullius. Aside from the alternative livery, the only noticeable difference was the roll bar — Group 44 used a full cockpit width version.

build a 'bitsa' from the remains of both.

1962 swung sharply from disaster to glory and the first of a number of SCCA titles that Tullius would accumulate over the years. In 1963 he left Kodak to join a Triumph agency based at Arlington Virginia and run by Walter Hutcherson, the man he credits with having done more than anyone to help him make a career in racing. That year he won another title and formed his first team: TGF Racing -Tullius, plus fellow Triumph racers Dick Gilmartin and Brian Fuerstenau.

The partnership with Gilmartin didn't endure but in 1965 Tullius formed Group 44 in association with engineering wizard Fuerstenau. The incorporated logo was a reversed 44 - at racing school Tullius had asked for a double digit number and someone had put 44 on backwards; it was as simple as that.

Group 44 was Tullius' team, but young Fuerstenau was left to look after the technical side while the boss concentrated on developing the operation as a promotional vehicle for its sponsors: "We had to pay the bills. Having been a salesman I knew that a properly presented team with its own built-in marketing and PR could promote someone's product effectively. In those days that was a new concept", he reflects.

Group 44 received parts and some cash from Triumph but Quaker State oil was its primary source of income and was to enjoy a long, fruitful relationship with it. While the team concentrated on running Triumph, and after the formation of British Leyland also MG sportscars, Tullius took his own driving career into other arenas. Winning the first ever professional Trans Am race at Daytona in 1967 in a Dodge Dart and joining the crew of a Howmet turbine powered prototype that raced at Le Mans in 1968 were among his exploits.

Aside from the upgraded Trans Am, SCCA road racing was essentially amateur. Nevertheless, there was precious little other sports car road racing on the North American continent so it received good media attention and drew healthy crowds. British Leyland's sportscar business was strong in the USA during the Sixties and early Seventies and SCCA competition 51

Jaguar V12 Race Cars

gave it a chance to pit its wares against those of its rivals. The 1974 B Production class pitted the E type against other imports like the Porsche 911SC and, most importantly, possibly the toughest showroom rival for the Jaguar, the home-brewed Chevrolet Corvette.

The Group 44 and Huffaker E types were secretly prepared and tested through the spring and summer of '74 and were formally announced only a short while before each made its race début over the weekend of 10/11 August. Group 44's car was driven by Tullius at Watkins Glen in a Northeastern Division race, while Huffaker's was piloted by Lee Mueller in a Western Division event at Seattle. It was a shock weekend for the Corvette equipped rivals, who

under normal circumstances would have expected to have had it all their own way. Mueller won his race and Tullius was leading comfortably when his gear lever broke. In 1974, the E type was the force to be reckoned with in B Production.

After dominating their respective regional championships, the two Jaguars met at the SCCA's 'Champion Spark Plug Road Racing Classic' - the national run-off meeting, held on Road Atlanta over the weekend of 2/3 November. Tullius captured the B Production pole, while Mueller lined up alongside.

The early stages of the race saw an impressive 1-2 formation held by the wailing V12 warriors, Tullius setting a new lap record as he stayed ahead of Mueller. But there was a surprise in store. While Mueller fell back with a slow puncture caused by an unscheduled off-road excursion, Tullius came under pressure from a Corvette driven by one Bill Jobe.

From the Mid Western Division, Jobe's Corvette was the first that either team had come

Early days — Tullius at Lime Rock in 1974. Note the neat twin exhaust and low 'windscreen'.

across which was capable of exerting such pressure. Through six regional events, Group 44 had never been pressed beyond the opening stages of a typical half hour race. Tullius' tyres went off and Jobe forced through to win by 0.8 seconds. Just to cap off the day, Fuerstenau's MGB was beaten, again by a whisker, by a Porsche in its class.

With regional titles again a formality the following season, Tullius went on to take the 1975 National crown; this year a broken differential cost Huffaker's chances. Tullius' national decider was his 12th win from 17 starts - a remarkable record when one considers that the Corvette had been racing successfully for so long that it had won 14 of the previous 17 years' national titles.

The Group 44 and Huffaker E types were developed independently and without any technical assistance from Jaguar, but came out very close in specification. Group 44's car was, of course, developed by Fuerstenau, an intuitive engineer with no formal training. He had only

been 21 years old when Tullius had spotted his talents, and Group 44 had lost him to the draft for a couple of years in the early days. In the early Seventies Group 44's engineering strength was reinforced by the recruitment of Lawton 'Lanky' Foushee as crew chief. A one-time Air Force One engineer (tending the presidential jet) turned NASCAR crew chief, 'Lanky' would go on to inherit the mantle of Group 44's engineering director when Fuerstenau eventually dissolved his partnership with Tullius to concentrate on special projects, many for Group 44.

"We finished our E type first and invited Huffaker to look over it", recalls Foushee, "but he didn't take advantage of our offer. Nevertheless, when we got together at the run-offs we

Lee Mueller gave the Huffaker Engineering E type its debut race at Seattle in August 1974. He shocked the Corvette regulars by easing to a convincing win.

Start of the 1974 B Production national run-off at Road Atlanta, headed by the two E types. Tullius is outdragging Mueller, who later dropped further away with a slow puncture. Tullius looked a good bet for victory until his tyres went off...

found we had come up with the same solutions to the same problems".

The cars (and there was only ever one built by each team) were tightly restricted in terms of the modifications permissible under SCCA B Production regulations. They were switched to heavy duty Koni spring-damper units at the rear and the manufacture of heavy duty front torsion bars was one of the few things that the two teams co-operated on. It wasn't found necessary to otherwise alter the standard wishbone suspension, which came complete with anti-roll bars front and back. However, Lanky recalls that Group 44 produced race quality hubs, widened the track front and rear with wheel offsets and naturally took advantage of the freedom to run 1½ in. wider than standard wheels. Goodyear slicks were fitted, as standard for B Production cars, 23½ x 11 x 15 at the front and 27 x 11 x 15 at the rear.

Stopping the fast but heavy car was a problem, the SCCA insisting on essentially standard brakes, which for the V12 E type were servo assisted discs, ventilated at the front. Additional cooling air ducts, alternative fluids and pads were areas of improvement for Group 44's racer, and the team ended up producing its own servo system in an attempt to get a sufficiently fast recovery time for racing. The servo was re-positioned in the cockpit to allow re-routing of the exhaust.

The SCCA E types carried steel roadster shells with flared arches. A mandatory roll over bar was added, but there wasn't any chassis strengthening. The SCCA allowed the hood and windscreen to be removed, the latter being replaced by a low perspex shield. The only aerodynamic appendage that was legal was a chin spoiler, which could not project out of the plan of the car. The E type didn't need any additional front downforce with the V12 lump in place, but the spoiler was found useful in improving cooling by increasing the pressure of air entering the radiator. The radiator itself was a non-standard item, a Harrison aluminium job developed for the Corvette, and was used without a fan as all starts were rolling.

Tullius in action in 1975 (above). This was the year of triumph at the Road Atlanta run-off (right), hence the jubilation shared by Mike Dale and the Group 44 crew.

A custom-made Serck oil cooler was mounted behind a headlamp opening. The engine had to be essentially standard, although the flywheel could be lightened and the exhaust was free, Group 44 developing its own six-into-one system for each bank. Forgetrue pistons were produced for both east and west V12s and both teams worked on normal blueprinting principles to obtain greater power. Group 44 reckons to have extracted 460 bhp on standard carburation.

Apart from jetting, there was nothing that could be done to improve the Stromberg set up,

in theory. In practice it was found difficult to get the carburettors working in unison under cornering. The cornering forces would make the fuel slosh around inside the chambers to the extent that one side's supply would be leaned off while the other side's would become over-rich. In the end the team had to develop its own baffle system to cut down the amount the fuel could slosh about. There was also a problem of oil sloshing about in the standard wet sump. The E type ran three times with a wet sump in testing, the baffling and pick up being progressively improved, but the team wasn't happy with it and after fighting with the problem for half a dozen races the switch was made to a dry sump. Foushee recalls, "keeping control of the oil in the standard long, shallow pan was almost impossible - we tried baffling with little success and were forced into dry sumping". The team developed its own dry sump, incorporating a Weaver Bros. pump.

The SCCA E types started out with a standard gearbox but it was later (accidentally) discovered that the factory had suitable close ratio gears which it had developed for a 4.2 litre six cylinder 2+2; these were duly supplied to the teams.

The racing E type's all-up weight was 2670 lb, which was close to that of a Corvette. The all-American rival was shorter in wheelbase and wider in track but the Jaguar handled just as well, though it was prone to be harder on tyres due to its narrower track. With a similar amount of power, its advantage lay in its lower frontal area - it was significantly faster in a straight line and its overall superiority was evident right from the word go.

Having so successfully exploited the E type over two seasons, by 1976 Tullius was raring to put the Jaguar V12's Corvette-beating potential to work in SCCA Professional racing. In 1975 the Trans-Am series, which embraced events throughout the USA and Canada, had been restructured to incorporate two categories, the less highly modified Category 1's regulations being based around those of B Production. By 1976 the E type had been phased out but the new XJ-S promised to be an equally effective means of exploiting the V12 in the new look Trans Am series. British Leyland Inc. agreed to support a B Production XJ-S aimed specifically at the 1976 amateur run-off, with a view to a Trans Am programme in 1977.

The XJ-S built by Group 44 in 1976 received similar modifications to the E type and an exploratory Trans Am outing was made at Mosport Park on 22nd August in the penultimate round of the 1976 series. The car had been under development from early spring and ran encouragingly until the single headlamp oil cooling set up proved inadequate in heavy traf-

fic. The extreme cockpit heat generated by the passenger seat mounted oil tank as well as heat soak from the engine also contrived against Tullius, the Group 44 chief dropping from seventh to tenth overall.

Given that it was running in the less highly modified class (Category 2 featuring European style Group 5 silhouette cars), the XJ-S' Trans Am début was highly encouraging. Following its Mosport début the car won three amateur races (taking its first win at Lime Rock) but at the Road Atlanta run-off Tullius spun on cold tyres at the first corner. He worked his way back up to fourth only for a carburettor plug to fall out causing a fire. Only prompt action by the corner workers saved the car.

Group 44's Trans Am XJ-S, like its E type, had essentially standard suspension, in this instance the road car featuring coil spring damper units (which were suitably uprated) both front and rear. However, the subframe had its normal rubber insulation removed to produce a more rigid structure. Group 44's in-house developed 9″ diameter front coils were three to four times stiffer than those of the production car.

Group 44 was allowed to equip the XJ-S with vented rear discs, inboard mounted on the XJ-S as on the E type, but a problem arose on this model with heat soak into the differential boiling the diff fluid. To overcome this the fluid had to be pumped through a small rear mounted oil cooler. The XJ-S had an ATL fuel cell in the lowest part of the boot, behind the rear axle, to keep the weight low and towards the rear. For the same reason the boot also accommodated the oil tank, battery and fire extinguisher.

Group 44's Trans Am effort spanned two years and during that period a number of different brake calipers were used, including an eight-pot caliper as developed for the ill-fated Broadspeed XJ12 coupé. This complex unit was designed to get a lot of pad area while avoiding tapering off the pads as they wore and it worked to a degree for the Trans Am effort. However, lack of spares forced the team back to a more conventional twin caliper, four pot system (using magnesium calipers), and this proved just as successful as it allowed a better air flow to the disc,

Lee Mueller puts the Huffaker E type through its paces. If his helmet is to be believed, he had a very modest opinion of his own driving skill!

which consequently ran cooler. In retrospect the eight-pot calipers were unnecessarily complex, once the team had mastered the trick of balancing the hydraulics to make the four pot, twin caliper system work properly.

Like the E type, the XJ-S was allowed a chin spoiler and this conferred the same, improved radiator cooling benefit. Indeed, it allowed the team to blank off a portion of the standard radiator opening, which improved straightline speed. With increasing engine power, the radiator itself was uprated to a Hurst aluminium NASCAR unit.

The key to improved engine performance was the SCCA's acceptance of a six Weber 44IDA carburettor set up, to replace the standard fuel injection introduced with the XJ-S. The Lucas-Bosch system was not race worthy so the team petitioned for the Weber kit, which was sold as an aftermarket item in the UK, knowing that better breathing was the secret of greater power. In agreeing to the Weber kit the SCCA, in Foushee's opinion, "unlocked the potential of the V12".

With similar preparation to the E type, the XJ-S raced with 530/540 bhp from the outset,

the power transmitted by the same close ratio gears as employed in the E type, in a different housing. In 1977, with a steel shell (only a fibreglass bonnet and plexiglass rear window saving weight), it was one of the heaviest cars in its class; around 3150 lb as against 2800 lb for a Corvette. Like the Corvette, it had a shorter (102 in.) wheelbase and wider track than the E type. On the mandatory 10 in. wide wheels it handled well and its power to weight ratio was competitive. Tullius loved the XJ-S - it had a more powerful engine, a better wheelbase to track ratio, wider wheels and power steering which made a one hour Trans Am race light work compared with the effort required of drivers of rival cars. The XJ-S wasn't as fast as the E type in a straight line due to its greater frontal area but it certainly had a handling advantage over its predecessor and was racing against other coupés.

The XJ-S won Category 1 in pouring rain at

Jaguar V12 Race Cars

Tullius switched to an XJ-S in 1976 and made it a winner in regional B Production events. It was intended for Trans Am races and made a highly encouraging debut in the professional series at Mosport in Canada.

on 30th May (finishing a splendid fourth overall) and went on to win the category at Westwood, Mosport Park and Road America. Tullius wound up as Category 1 Champion, narrowly defeating Porsche 911SC driver John Bauer who took only two victories but amassed four second places and three other top four placings while Tullius backed up his wins with one second, one third and one fourth.

More often than not there had been a strong Porsche presence at the front of Category 1, the German marque represented by a number of quick drivers. It claimed the Manufacturers title thanks to its strength in numbers. The 911SC produced around 450 bhp, but was considerably lighter than the XJ-S at around 1850 lb. and Bauer's efforts were backed up by those of Tom Spalding and John Wood, both of whom won races. However, Jaguar left the Corvette trailing in the marque standings.

After a season of Porsche success in both Trans Am categories, the SCCA revised its rules for 1978 and the Corvette became a better proposition in Category 1. However, the Jaguar maintained its competitiveness, thanks to more power and less weight, and 1978 became another Jaguar versus Corvette affair.

The V12's power increased progressively over the '77 and '78 seasons from 530 to 560 bhp partly due to camshaft and cylinder head

In 1977 Tullius moved into professional racing, chasing the Trans Am series. His effort was fully professional thanks to support from long standing sponsors Quaker State Oil and British Leyland.

development, the SCCA allowing the removal but not the addition of metal. Wilder camshafts saw the rev limit taken up to 8000 rpm. The exhaust system was also improved, larger diameter, shorter primary pipes plumbed to a single pipe each side (rather than twin pipes either side) providing a hefty extra 100 bhp at 4000 rpm.

The '78 car was lighter than its '77 predecessor thanks to an aluminium roll cage and an acid dipped bodyshell. Foushee says that the shell was discovered at Coventry, having been one of a batch of six prepared for a second-generation Broadspeed project that never came to fruition. The job had been done properly, the structural members having been set aside before the dip and welded into place afterwards. The '78 XJ-S also benefited from a GRP boot lid and GRP wings. In other respects it represented an extension of what had been learnt with the '77 car. An interesting development that appeared during the 1978 season was a brake water cooling system. A Lucas fuel injection nozzle was mounted behind each disc to squirt water which would evaporate and carry the heat away. The nozzle was fed by a Lucas fuel injection pump, actuated by a stop light switch under the driver's command. Tighter courses required as much as four gallons to last the first half of a typical one hour race, during which the fuel load was heavy.

The '78 Jaguar, despite its lighter chassis, was still around 200 lb. heavier than the Corvette, which, with 550 bhp on tap in 1978, was gradually overhauled by the XJ-S in the power stakes. The British car was reckoned to have a handling superiority, but the two major contenders were closely matched. The '78 season started in Chevrolet's favour but after three successive defeats (the first due to a rare engine failure, caused by a broken cam follower), Group 44 "got its act together" as Foushee puts it, and

went on to win the remaining seven races. Not by E type style domination, but by hard graft. Tullius' drivers title, captured by a healthy points margin, was hard fought and well won.

"It was a lot of work, a tough season", Foushee recalls, and although Tullius pulled away in the points race, the Corvette's numerical superiority kept Chevrolet well in the hunt for the manufacturers accolade. In response, Group 44 prepared the heavier '77 car, uprated where possible to '78 specification, and entered it in the last two races of the season, for Fuerstenau.

Group 44's engineer had already finished first at Watkins Glen, by sharing with Tullius in the World Championship of Makes six hour enduro which was included in the '78 Trans Am schedule. The pair collected a fine seventh overall in this unusually long event. Fuerstenau went on to collect third at Laguna Seca and, hampered by a broken hub, eighth at Mexico City, which vaulted him to fourth in the points chart and helped secure the manufacturers crown for Jaguar.

The 1977 Trans Am XJ-S. Tullius at the wheel. Note the neater, wider one piece front spoiler used this season.

Bob Tullius in full flight, the British Leyland/Quaker State XJ-S en route for the Category 1 Championship. Alas, Porsche's numerical superiority cost Jaguar the manufacturers' crown.

Jaguar V12 Race Cars

Sadly, the marque was having far less success on the commercial front at this stage and Group 44 continued to serve Leyland over the '79 and '80 seasons by racing the Triumph TR8 in the IMSA GTO series. The Trans Am's prestige had declined by the end of the Seventies and IMSA offered a better, more competitive and more prestigious championship. For the Eighties, IMSA introduced prototypes, producing an American equivalent of Europe's Group C, while the SCCA concentrated on production cars with a revamped Trans Am series. Tullius, as recounted elsewhere in these pages, successfully sold the concept of a V12

The 1981 Trans Am XJ-S (below and right) was a tube frame car clothed in Jaguar panels. The V12 engine was shifted back 8″ which improved traction and the space-frame chassis gave the car greater all-round ability.

powered prototype to
the newly independent Jaguar in late
1980, and was set to work to tackle the 1981
Trans Am with a new style XJ-S as a filler.

The 1981 programme came as a last minute reprieve for a team that was being disbanded, the Triumph TR8 having been phased out and the commercial performance of Leyland having declined to the extent that any sort of racing looked out of the question. When the never-say-die Tullius finally sold the prototype concept to the newly independent Jaguar, to be given confirmation of an interim Trans Am project, he had little time to work with.

The new style Trans Am called for a new type of XJ-S. The series was now based around a single category and allowed liberal modification under the skin, to the extent that the standard monocoque could be replaced by a tubular frame hung with standard shape metal panels. Between February and April 1981 Group 44 built its own spaceframe, to which were attached the '78

Category 1 XJ-S's dipped steel panels. The team discovered that aluminium doors, bonnet and boot lid had been produced in Coventry and these were duly acquired.

A familiar air dam adorned the front (and the oil radiators were still in the headlamp openings) but a novelty was the use of a rear spoiler, now Trans Am legal. The spaceframe car had familiar twin caliper four pot brakes and still had to run on 10 in. wide wheels. It used standard XJ-S control arms and uprights at the front and a standard live rear axle, albeit with the lower control arms modified to allow camber adjustment at the outer rather than the inner ends. The car ran softly sprung with a fair amount of body roll and the geometry was altered to reduce camber change in view of the lower aspect ratio tyres and wider wheels available in 1981. The rules allowed the engine to be moved back until the furthest forward spark plug was in line with the front wheels. This gave Group 44 8 in. of rearward shift and as the V12 was already 10 in. longer than a Chevrolet V8 that put the transmission a full 18 in. further back than in 65 rival cars. Even dry, the car was heavier on its rear than on its front wheels, and the wheelspin that had sometimes been induced by the '77/78 cars was a thing of the past. The '81 XJ-S's improved weight distribution allowed it to run a softer front anti-roll bar and softer front tyres than the opposition. Its drivetrain was lifted directly from the '78 Mexico winning car. Over the '81 season the team had a fresh look at the engine and through camshaft and cylinder head development increased power from 560 to 570 bhp.

By 1981 the V12 could run 8000 rpm regularly - in the past the engine had only exceeded 7500 rpm if absolutely necessary. Three hours continuous running at 8000 rpm was sure to break a valve spring. By 1981 lighter titanium valves, easier cam profiles, better valve springs and better valve cooling through increased oil splash had allowed 8000 rpm to be run safely, even throughout a six hour race. Only for 12 and 24 hour races were revs reduced - to just below 7000 rpm.

The car was heavier than the Corvette - a 5.3 litre Corvette was allowed to run at 2700 lb. whereas the XJ-S had to carry 200 lb more. This SCCA imposed weight penalty was imposed on the basis of the XJS's Webers and i.r.s.

The first year of the new look Trans Am, 1980, had seen John Bauer collect the title in another Porsche 911 derivative, but by the end of the year Greg Pickett had clearly had the fastest car - a Corvette. New entries for 1981 included factory supported Porsche 924 Turbos but it was a Corvette built in Canada by Brad Francis for veteran Eppie Weitzes that would provide the main opposition for Tullius.

Former Formula 5000 Champion Weitzes had been on the sidelines for five years when he arrived at Charlotte for the opening round. Nevertheless, he managed to pip Tullius by a fraction of a second to be declared winner after on-the-road victor George Follmer (Camaro) had been penalized 15 seconds for passing under caution flags. Weitzes had a series lead that he wouldn't relinquish. Nevertheless, Tullius would win more races, three to two. Despite its weight penalty and with little development

work, the XJ-S regularly ran in the top three - a lower end of the top six position was only seen on the odd off day. Alas Tullius hit trouble on three occasions, while Weitzes posted only one DNF. At Sears Point a broken distributor jack shaft cost a likely second place, at Lime Rock an overheating gearbox dropped the car down to fourth but a malfunctioning fuel valve caused retirement in the late stages while at Trois Rivieres a broken valve spring caused an early retirement. In the hotly contested '81 series, those retirements were crucial. Consistency won the title; by way of consolation Group 44 took the accolade of the "winningest team".

Tullius' first win came in the second round at Portland, Oregon, a course on which the V12 could stretch its legs. After practice bothers he lined up 14th on the grid but came through to notch up his first outright professional race win since Daytona 1967. Rather than take the victory lap, he pulled into the pits to share the occasion with Lanky and the lads.

Tying on points after the first two rounds was the closest Tullius got to Weitzes in the season's table. Nevertheless, he went on to win rounds five and seven at Brainerd and Mosport Park, after which the gearbox hampered his efforts to stop the Corvette driver. Continuing engine development was putting too great a strain on the standard Jaguar 'box.

Gearbox problems blighted a run for the XJ-S in IMSA's 1982 early season Daytona 24 Hour event. The car was run on street radials at the instigation of Goodyear and Tullius shared the driving with future prototype co-pilot Bill Adam and Gordon Smiley, who was set to take over the car for the '82 Trans Am series with backing from Intermedics. Having helped bring the gearbox-problem-delayed car home at Daytona, Smiley tragically lost his life at Indianapolis, one week before the Trans Am opener at Road Atlanta. Tullius stepped into the breach for that race but withdrew the entry for the rest of the season. The much more exciting prototype project was now on the boil.

JAGUAR V12

The Broadspeed XJ12C

It was in March 1976 that Leyland Cars dropped a bombshell on the motor racing world. At a press conference in London the organisation announced that it was to return to competition with a Jaguar works team. The announcement was greeted with great enthusiasm. The name Jaguar conjured up the great days of racing in the 1950s at a time when the British motor industry was at a low ebb.

Ralph Broad and his highly respected Broadspeed preparation company would be preparing two XJ12 coupés for the European Touring Car Championship. The team would run in red, white and blue livery with sponsorship from Jaguar's parent. It was to be an all-British effort, and right from the word go, it was made clear that the team was going out to win. Derek Bell, David Hobbs, Andy Rouse and Steve Thompson were to drive the powerful machines. What could possibly go wrong?

Leyland was expecting an instant miracle, an answer to all its problems. Success would restore prestige in the market place, would motivate and inspire the workforce and the dealer networks. It was an instant Eldorado.

The British press and public jumped at the idea. The confidence was translated to the people, and they expected success. When it did not come immediately the project became a curious sideshow: the cars were always quick, but could they survive and win? Time and time again, they

failed and eventually after 18 months Leyland announced that the experiment was over. In the racing team there was disappointment and almost a sense of relief. The pressure had been too much right from the start. The victories which the PR men had promised in March 1976 had never come, but the car had progressed. "I remember being very disappointed when they pulled out," says Andy Rouse, "The company was naïve I suppose, they expected too much, too soon. They had promised success, and it never came. They could have had all the success they wanted in 1978. We needed time to develop away some of the problems of the car. If we had been able to do that, the car would have won every race in the European series."

If the XJ12 coupé did not live up to expectations, it was nonetheless a formidable racing machine. The team had all the power it needed from the V12 engine but the car was too heavy, the development time too short, and the publicity too great. It was a mistake which the highly sucessful Tom Walkinshaw Racing Jaguar XJ-S team avoided. It came quietly into racing, without any boasts and as the car improved, so did the publicity. It might not have stolen the same headlines at the start of the project, but by the end it had proved what the XJ12C project had failed to do. Jaguar did have the potential to beat the best in Europe.

In 1975 when the decision to return to rac- 67

ing was made, the British motor industry was in disarray. The energy crisis had hit hard. It was a time when fuel efficiency was becoming all important, and the big luxury car days were coming to an end. The XJ12C project was a bold attempt to regain some of the confidence of the 1960s and early 1970s.

Leyland management stressed from the very early days that it was not for the love of the sport that it had returned Jaguar to the race tracks. Jaguar's rivals had gained a great deal of publicity and prestige from the success in the European Touring Car series, most notably BMW which had dominated the series in the early 1970s. The racing project was seen from the start as a good sound marketing policy in an effort to increase sales.

Many people were surprised that Jaguar had not returned to sports car racing, a field which had seen so much success for the company in the 1950s. Why did the corporate marketing men choose to race saloons?

Saloon car racing has always been the closest of all areas of the sport to the public. The cars raced are not merely racing 'specials'. A gulf that developed between the motor industry and the sport was bridged by saloons; recognisable machines, to which the man in the street was able to aspire. There is little doubt that Leyland's philosophy was correct. If the Jaguars had won the corporation's image would have been enhanced and sales would have increased. The problem was that they chose the wrong car.

When the idea was first discussed by Ralph Broad and Leyland Cars' Motor Sports liaison manager, Simon Pearson, they had considered running the lighter XJ-S model. But again the marketing men won the day. The XJ12C looked more like a traditional high performance touring

The Broadspeed XJ12 coupe was not really ready to race in 1976 but having been announced early in the year and continually scratched from events, British Leyland had to put on some sort of a show at the Silverstone TT, come late September. Derek Bell put the Big Cat on pole but after 14 laps half shaft failure confined her to her lair.

car and was considered to be closer to the public image of what a Jaguar was. The XJ-S was a new car, less well known and less recognisable as a Jaguar. The decision was taken, and there was no going back. By the middle of 1977, when the XJ12Cs were not enjoying the success that had been expected, there was talk of a switch to the XJ-S, and a certain amount of preparatory work was done behind the scenes, but by then the team and the company really had no course but to continue; they could not afford to lose face.

The basic philosophy behind the project was business and an increase of confidence and sales in Leyland products. The marketing team had grasped the importance of the sport in relation to the sales of cars and there is no doubt that the organisation took a bold step indeed. Alas, what it failed to grasp was that, no matter how good an engine and no matter how good the drivers were, these things take time. Expansive publicity, too early in the project, meant that there was no time. Patience was an expensive commodity. In the end the Broadspeed XJ12Cs took too

long, and were needlessly consigned to a backwater in saloon car racing history ....

It was Ralph Broad who, more than anyone, was responsible for the birth of the exciting but ill-fated project. From 1974 onwards he had been preparing highly successful British based Triumph Dolomite Sprints for Leyland, while at the same time continually pushing for a Jaguar to be used in the European series. His company, based at Southam, was the most celebrated saloon and engine specialist firm in Britain, with a long record of success dating back to the early 1960s.

Broadspeed had begun in 1959, but it was not until 1964 that the company leapt to prominence with a pair of Mini Coopers driven by John Fitzpatrick and John Handley. Running

Testing at Silverstone in 1976, the XJ12C gave the Broadspeed lads plenty to scratch their heads about. The development of a competitive ETCC racer was a long and often painful process and was sadly a task that was not to be completed...

against works opposition the cars scored some notable successes in 1964 and 1965 before Broadspeed turned its attention to preparing Ford Anglias with factory backing.

John Fitzpatrick won the British Championship for Ford in 1966 and was just pipped at the post in the 1967 series by the Falcon of Frank Gardner. A switch to Ford Escorts brought further successes in the following two years with John Fitzpatrick again behind the wheel, partnered on this occasion by Chris Craft.

Keith Greene joined the team for the 1970 season, bringing with him a wealth of experience in saloon car racing to help prepare more Escorts. The same year Andy Rouse began an association with the company which was to last until the late Seventies. In 1980 the company finally went into liquidation.

The link with Ford was to continue until the 1974 season with Capris and Escorts being prepared for both the works team and privateers. At the end of 1973, however, Broad was approached by John Barber, the managing director of British Leyland and was subsequently contracted to develop and race works Dolomite Sprints. Rouse and Tony Dron dominated the 2500 cc class of the Group One national championship.

By this stage, Rouse had taken over the running of the Broadspeed competition department, proving himself to be a fine test and race driver and a gifted organiser.

From the start of the Dolomite Sprint days Broad had been talking to Leyland about the possibility of running a Jaguar in the Group Two European Touring Car series, and with new, more relaxed regulations due at the start of the 1976 season it seemed a good time to embark on the project.

Once the factory had given Broadspeed the go-ahead in October 1975, it was five months before the first prototype was ready to run. The plan was to run an all-British car from the body shell right down to the ancillaries. Ralph Broad and his design team of David Griffiths and Roger King spent a month deciding exactly what they wanted before work began.

The standard two door XJ bodyshell was first lightened, although through its short career the car remained very heavy for a Group Two racer. Reinforcing took the form of a strong roll cage, and strengthened front and rear bulkheads.

The most notable changes to the bodywork were the neat flared wheel arches, extending four inches on either side of the car to the maximum permissible width. Over the winter of 1976/77 these were totally altered to accommodate 19in. rather than the original 16in. wheels. The 1977 spec cars also featured redesigned spoilers, with a rubber rear spoiler which did not appear on the prototype.

The balance of the car impressed the drivers from the very early days, the weight distribution of the standard car being little altered in the racing machine. "It wasn't particularly difficult to drive," remembers Andy Rouse, "but it was a physical car. For such a heavy car it drove well."

Under the bonnet the massive flat head V12 engine was bored out by a 0.6 mm, the legal maximum, giving it a capacity of 5410 cc, which was capable of producing in excess of 560 bhp. Special pistons were forged for the team by Cosworth Engineering, featuring redesigned crowns to create an alternative combustion chamber. Changes to the shape of the crowns and the head itself took place over the winter of 1976/77 and several different combustion shapes were tried. Designed to run with a compression ratio of 12:1, Broadspeed's engine employed larger than standard inlet and exhaust valves. The regulations dictated that the crankshaft be standard, but the con rods were custom designed and matched by X-ray. The cam shafts were machined from solid, by Broadspeed.

The engine was inclined back at two degrees and moved slightly rearwards to allow more space for the larger racing ancillaries and the standard Jaguar lubrication system was modified in an attempt to keep the oil to the rear of the engine where the oil pump was situated. The engine was so long that under braking the oil surged forward and starved the pump. The standard design had just one rear sump, but Broadspeed fitted a second nearer the front of the engine to try to combat the oil surge.

In the initial stages of development it was oil 71

The improved 1977 XJ12C (above and below) was a racer that didn't fulfil its potential. Continuing development work ironed out many of the early bugs but the programme needed another year if it was to succeed. Note the front splitter — a device more commonly seen on formula cars and prototypes. This divides the airflow above and below the car and provides a measure of downforce.

surge, more than anything else which delayed progress, and it was not until the team had tried a considerable number of sump configurations that it was able to begin to combat the problem. At Monza in 1977 the team tried a system which included a reserve tank which fed oil under gas pressure to enable it to keep the engine supplied with oil under braking. When in mid '77 the CSI allowed the use of dry sumps, a system was tried on one of the cars, but it was never fully developed before the cars were withdrawn from competition. By the end of 1977 the development of various oil scavenge systems seemed to be working better with each race. Dry sumping might have been more successful, but as the Group A XJ-S was to prove later on, it was not essential. The oil surge problem remained Broadspeed's Achilles Heel throughout, but there is little doubt that with a little more time to develop its wet sump system

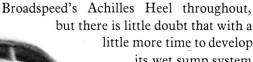

the problem would ultimately have been solved.

Cooling, too, proved to be a problem early on in the project. The front of the cars featured a standard grille and a wider unit beneath it. The upper grille supplied air to the very large oil cooler, while the lower grille fed air to a large Broadspeed designed, Serck-manufactured water radiator as well as the front brakes and dampers. For 1977 this was altered and the brakes were fed via air scoops.

The brakes of the prototype were single caliper four pot systems, but due to the weight of the car these were later switched for twin calipers working on the AP alloy discs; in early tests the brake fluid had boiled. Long periods of hard braking did not suit the car and its performance on tight circuits was never impressive. At the rear, unlike the later European XJ-S, the brakes were mounted inboard and cooled by air duct. This tended to trap heat close to the transmission and drive systems which was to cause serious damage on occasion despite the use of a diff fluid cooler. Plans to cool the brakes with blowers during pitstops only served to underline that the inboard system was not the most effective.

Interestingly, in 1977 there was talk of using water injection to cool the brake discs in the early laps of the race, but unlike Group 44, Broadspeed did not develop a system.

Lucas supplied the ignition and fuel injection systems, there being an electrical system for starting the car and a mechanical system for when the car was in motion.

The exhaust featured three-into-one pipes which were designed by Andy Rouse and which fed pipes that emerged on either side of the car behind the doors. The system gave the car its distinctive roar which still induces bouts of nostalgia among the people involved with the project when it is mentioned.

The gearbox was a standard Jaguar manual four speed unit with its own oil cooler mounted underneath the car at the right rear corner, with the corresponding cooler for the diff on the left handside.

Steering of the XJ12 was power assisted but this did not seem to distress the drivers in the least, all those who drove it commenting on how good it felt at really high speeds.

There remained the problem of fuel consumption, but as with the later ETCC XJ-S, Broad and his men were able to derive a balance whereby the car was quick enough to pull clear of the opposition to allow itself time for the extra pitstops. The sad fact was that there were very few occasions upon which the team managed to get as far as that first scheduled stop.

As the PR men were telling the world that they had a car that would sweep all before it in the European Touring Car Championship, Ralph Broad and his men at Southam had completed just one car, although there was a second on the way. The international homologation without which the cars could not race was not due until 1st April 1976, which meant that whatever happened the team would have to miss the opening round of the series at Monza in Italy. Testing had been severely curtailed by the appalling weather in the early months of the

Andy Rouse hustles the 1977 XJ-S around Silverstone (above and right). The Broadspeed engineer/driver played a key role in the development of British Leyland's ETCC challenger. He firmly believes only time cost the project success.

75

year, but it was clear as soon as the car turned a wheel that there was a considerable amount of work still to be done before the cars could race.

Several weeks were spent at Goodwood, but the rain never seemed to stop. Andy Rouse had managed but two days of dry testing but was nevertheless enthusiastic about the car. "It was a very frustrating time," he remembers, "we were unable to get any genuine testing to gather information and try out new parts. It was not an easy car to drive, but it handled quite well and of course the horsepower was incredible."

The main problems, however, concerned the wet sump the car had to use to comply with the Group Two regulations. It was a problem which was to remain until well into 1977.

The bad weather continued until April and a week after the Monza race Leyland announced that the début of the car had been put back to 2nd May at Mugello, rather than at the Salzburgring on Easter Monday. The little testing that had been done revealed that there was still a great deal of work to be done on the suspension, the brakes and, of course, the oil feed problem.

In the press the news was greeted with a certain cynicism, and as the year progressed through the long hot summer of 1976 the headlines repeated time and again that the race début had been further delayed. Come late September and the Silverstone Tourist Trophy, the car had to appear. It was still not really ready, and still very much a prototype machine. Nevertheless, the home crowd was appeased when Derek Bell took pole position on qualifying tyres with a time of 1 min. 36.72 sec., almost two seconds ahead of the nearest BMW. On the warm up lap the Jaguar was applauded all the way round the Northamptonshire circuit. The crowd had come, and expected great things. After battling with the leading BMW for 14 laps the car suffered a half shaft failure, which at the time was blamed on a puncture. It was to be the first of many failures of that kind.

The Silverstone TT was to be the car's only race of 1976, but in January the company announced that 1977 would see a two car team in all events, and that the cars would be con-

The 1977 TT was the final straw for the Broadspeed project. Success on home soil might well have saved the programme for another year, but Schenken/Fitzpatrick (seen in the pits) lost a wheel and Rouse (right) spun off on oil just ten laps from the end, when victory looked within grasp.

77

The early stages of the crucial 1977 TT race. Schenken leads Rouse and Quester into Copse. Neither Jaguar saw the finish: the BMW (shared with Walkinshaw) came through to win.

siderably different to the prototype version. The driver line-up too had changed Andy Rouse and Derek Bell being joined by John Fitzpatrick and Tim Schenken. There were new spoilers front and rear and 19in. wheels to replace the 16in. wheels used at the TT with the wheel arches redesigned to cope with these.

The revitalised team travelled first to Monza to discover that three new chicanes had sprung up. At such a fast circuit the addition of the new chicanes meant that the cars had to brake hard from high speed three times a lap. Come official

practice, the oil shot forward in the sumps and the engines deprived of oil, gave up. Broadspeed had no choice but to withdraw one car and hope for the best. John Fitzpatrick had nevertheless qualified his XJ12 on pole position, with a modified oil system fitted by means of a reserve tank and gas pressure to sustain the necessary flow of oil to the engine. For the first 45 minutes of the race Fitzpatrick led, before the oil gremlins struck again.

A month later the cars were out again at the Salzburgring and the oil problem seemed to have been solved thanks to Rouse testing and redesigning the sumping system. The brake problems, too, seemed to have finally gone away. What remained now was a problem of fuel consumption, the heavy Jaguar having to pit more often than the more nimble and light BMWs.

"We could have cruised around all day long, by that stage," recalls Rouse, "but with the consumption problem we had to go almost two seconds a lap quicker than the BMWs to make up for the extra stop we had to make. We had to drive harder, and then the cars broke more easily."

For the third time in its three race history the Jaguar had pole position, this time Bell taking the honour. This time it was Rouse's turn to lead, in the other car. Half an hour into the race it was all over again. Tim Schenken in the pole position car had pitted early on, worried by his rear suspension, and when Rouse came in with a holed radiator, checks revealed that all was not well with his suspension either. The heavy duty rear wheel flange forgings were wrongly grained and had sheared. With only a fortnight between

races there was not time to prepare new components and test them. The team waited in vain out in Europe in the hope of new parts before packing up and heading for home; they would miss the next two races at Mugello and Enna. The catalogue of disaster was continuing.

The team fought back at Brno in June, taking pole position once again, with everything back in order. Down the straights of the extremely rapid circuit they were hitting 170 mph. Brno, though, is a hard circuit on cars with the bumpy track upsetting stability and throwing up unexpected problems. Bell was in early in the race with a split oil pipe, and was to retire later with a gearbox problem, and the Fitzpatrick/Rouse car picked up a puncture early on a lap and had to struggle round the circuit to the pits; the flailing rubber all but destroyed the rear corner of the car. It was an hour before either car re-emerged from the pits. Fitzpatrick and Rouse struggled on through the afternoon to finally bring the car to the finish - its first - in a lowly 16th place.

A disastrous weekend at the Nurburgring saw a mammoth effort by the Broadspeed mechanics, changing the engines no fewer than five times. There was another pole position, one lap was easy enough, and Fitzpatrick duly led the field away, only to see the oil pressure drop. He was out, but Bell/Rouse continued, to take second place. It looked as if, finally, they were on the right track. Zandvoort saw a dry sump car for the first time; the Fitzpatrick/Schenken car was fitted with the untried system which was to fail four times in the race, while the wet sumped car of Rouse and Bell was once more up with the leaders until it, too, suffered an oil pump failure. The Fitzpatrick/Schenken car spent much of the afternoon in the pits, but eventually made it to the finish - unclassified.

The turning point in the Jaguar story came at Silverstone, a year after its début. Success was essential. The two XJ12Cs filled the front row and battled with the leading BMW until Schenken's wheel came adrift, and then just 10 laps from the end, Rouse's car hit oil and spun into the bank at Abbey. There was renewed optimism, but a week later, after a disastrous day at 79

Zolder, it was all over. Leyland announced that the cars would not be continuing.

As an exercise in engineering, the Jaguar XJ12 Coupé had not been a failure. Right from the very first days of the project Ralph Broad and his team had known that the car was overweight and that it used too much fuel, but as they developed the car they began to find, as they had suspected, that it did have the potential, if only they could iron out the problems.

Sadly, the project is more of a story of a marketing policy that went very wrong - a classic case of what *not* to do when going motor racing. In the end it was not through any glaring engineering failure that the whole car was finally shelved. The publicity men had promised publicity. They received it, and it was all bad. There was little choice left other than to get out of the sorry mess.

The promises of immediate success had naturally brought pressure to bear on Ralph Broad, who was perpetually fighting a battle against time. Despite all his years of experience not even he could turn the XJ12 into a winner overnight. The project was delayed at every turn and its progress, particularly in 1976, was painfully slow to watch. Through it all the Broadspeed men never gave up, facing each problem with renewed vigour. They knew the car could be a success, they just wanted to prove it.

The man at the centre of it all, Broad, suffered a tragic loss in the summer of 1977 when his 20 year old daughter was killed in a road accident. It was a devastating blow. He worked on throughout, soaking up the pressures which grew on him as the year progressed. The balance between success and failure is narrow indeed. Come September and the Tourist Trophy at Silverstone, what would have happened if there had been no patch of oil on the circuit at Abbey? If Rouse had not spun off and had gone on to beat Walkinshaw's BMW? It would have been a glorious home win. Perhaps the Leyland marketing men would have continued with the project and the cars would have gone on to win everything in 1978.

There are many who believe that the project was ill-conceived from the start, that the car would never have been a winner in Group 2. Broad, a man who surely could have spotted a winning potential in a car, was convinced that it could succeed. Rouse firmly believes that the coupés would have swept all before them. To drive, they were quick and stable on the fast circuits, although clearly never suited to the tight confines of twisty tracks. Before judging, take a look at the statistics. The cars competed in only eight events in all, and were on pole position for six of them. Had not everyone been told that the cars were going to win everything, it would have been an impressive record.

The story remains a painful one for Jaguar, but one which taught them well when Tom Walkinshaw, the man who had humbled the great coupés at Silverstone in 1977, came along to discuss the possibilities of running the XJ-S in Europe.

JAGUAR V12

The T.W.R. XJ-S

Tom Walkinshaw was fed up with racing foreign cars when he decided to 'Buy British' in 1979. After successes in Britain with the Austin Rover Vitesse, he turned his attention to finding a car that would be capable of beating the continental marques in the European Touring Car Championship.

"At the time", recalls Walkinshaw, "it was something of a national pastime to take the mickey out of British Leyland. They were even doing it themselves. No-one seemed to be worried by the fact that if the British motor industry failed they would not have a job to do." At a meeting in 1980 with the men at British Leyland, Walkinshaw commented that he thought the Jaguar XJ-S would be a good car to take on the might of BMW when the regulations were changed for Group A racing. Everyone thought he was joking.

That year Michael Edwardes handed control of Jaguar to Egan and a rebirth of the company began under its own control. The Leyland days were effectively over.

The more Walkinshaw and his team looked at the idea, the more they began to feel that the XJ-S did have the potential they were looking for, and eventually Walkinshaw approached the company and put the idea to Egan.

After the disasters of the Broadspeed cars in 1976-77 there was, not unnaturally, some suspicion among some of the people at Jaguar. They had burned their fingers once and were not going to let it happen again. Egan, however, saw the potential of the project and towards the end of 1981 gave TWR the go ahead.

This time there was no great splash of publicity. Throughout the winter the XJ-S was prepared at the TWR base at Kidlington in Oxfordshire and it was not until January that the press began to smell a story. "We let them think that we were doing it for Bathurst, because the car had been homologated for the Australian Group One series. Hence, the Australian Jag was born."

The low key approach was clearly the best policy. The pressures which had crippled the Broadspeed project from its very beginnings were avoided, leaving the team to work on the car and make it fully competitive. It took time, but unlike Broadspeed, Walkinshaw had time to play with.

From the very beginning the development of the XJ-S was left up to the men at Kidlington. Jim Randle, Jaguar's director of engineering, gave the team any assistance it wanted, but the project was financed by the Motul Oil Company.

The car proved it was a winner in the summer of 1982 and the following year the TWR crew fielded two cars, backed officially by the factory. Jaguar had a works team in Europe again. As success came, so the exposure of the 81

car was developed. The project gathered momentum. Jaguar was beginning to show to the world that it had a car that was as good as anything in Europe, and there were results to back up the boasts.

1984 saw further development of the same theme. The cars ran in the company's colours, British racing green. Britain, at last, had the national team it had longed for with the Broadspeed cars. And, the national team was winning. By the end of the year Walkinshaw had won the European title and the XJ-S had reached the very peak of its development. The three car team had travelled the circuits of Europe with astounding success: seven wins in twelve races, including two perfect 1-2-3 results, and on only two occasions the Jags had not been as high on the grid as was possible.

The racing was exciting too, the heavy Jaguars having to make an extra pitstop for fuel while the nimble BMWs could keep going. The drivers produced some memorable charges back to the front. There were occasional problems, but after three seasons in Europe the team was well drilled and experienced enough to handle them quickly and efficiently.

"We were out there, in British racing green," remembers the team boss, "racing for Britain and proud of it. Jaguar were behind us fully, they weren't hiding anymore and the success obviously had a knock-on effect on the public, the workforce and the dealer networks around the world."

Jaguar had got the equation right, thanks to a far-sighted executive and an ambitious Scotsman ....

Tom Walkinshaw's was a well known name around the tracks of Europe, but it was with the XJ-S that he achieved his greatest recognition as a driver *and* as a preparation specialist and team manager.

First appearance on home soil for the TWR XJ-S at Donington in 1982. Walkinshaw shows that the car is a force to be reckoned with by leading powerful Chevrolet and BMW opponents.

Walkinshaw began racing in his native Scotland in the late Sixties. Having won the Scottish Formula Ford title in a Hawke, he headed south in 1970 to compete in the British Formula Three championship, initially with a privately run Lotus and later in a works March. The year ended in a bad accident. Over the next three years Walkinshaw tried to advance his single seater career in Formula Three, Formula Two, Formula Atlantic and Formula 5000, in which he was the first man to take on the Chevrolets with the Ford V6 engine.

Lack of money led him in 1973 to take up saloon car racing while he continued to try and progress in formula car racing. After a couple of runs in a Nissan he aquired a Ford Escort and it was Ford who came to his rescue the following year, signing him up to test, develop and drive a three litre Capri in the British Saloon Car Championship. He duly won his class. His relationship with Ford was to continue through until 1977 when he joined BMW after some promising runs in the 1976 season in the Group 5 Hermetite BMW 3.5 CSL.

With BMW came more success, both at home and abroad. Partnering Dieter Quester, Walkinshaw won the 1977 Silverstone Tourist Trophy, and in doing so beat the Broadspeed Jaguars in front of their home crowd. 1978 saw Walkinshaw turning his attention to the European Touring Car series full time, winning the events at Brands Hatch and Jarama.

By this time Walkinshaw was tired of driving for other people and decided to set up his own preparation business, Tom Walkinshaw Racing. Continuing his links with BMW, he was the force behind the BMW County Challenge and it was TWR that prepared the 16 identical BMW323i's which were raced by celebrity drivers up and down the country. At the same time he was preparing Mazda RX7s for the British Saloon Car series. He won his class that year, and the following year signed up Win Percy to drive one of the rotary engined cars. Success followed success, and with it came a string of manufacturers keen for TWR to prepare their cars. The Rover Vitesse proved a startling success, before Walkinshaw turned his attention to 83

Jaguar V12 Race Cars

Europe with Jaguar.

While the XJ-S was still in its infancy the Rovers were winning in Britain, and by the summer of 1984 TWR was running five, and on occasion six, cars in the ETCC - Jaguars and Rovers.

The organisation continued to grow, branching out into rallying. TWR was, quite simply, the most professional outfit in the business. The standard in the European series was set by TWR.

The European Touring Car Championship had taken on a new lease of life with the introduction of Group A regulations at the start of 1982. The new rules endeavoured to bring racing saloons closer to standard machinery and away from the strange evolution devices that had existed in the Group Two Championship. Gone were the ungainly bulging wheel arches and spoilers. Aerodynamic aids in Group A had to be homologated, having first been fitted to the necessary 5000 cars destined for the showrooms. The brakes, drive system, gearbox and suspension were all free, although the suspension had to be fitted to the existing mounting points on the standard model.

On the engine front the specification of pistons, camshafts and other engine internals was free, although restrictions were placed on inlet size and valve lift and, more importantly for the Jaguar, the original cast exhaust manifold had to be retained.

Having studied the regulations, Walkinshaw knew he was looking for a car with the widest possible tyres, independent suspension and fuel injection. The XJ-S matched these demands, and although still a heavy car, with its limit of 1400 kg, it was just what TWR was looking for.

Outwardly the cars were little changed in appearance from the standard Jaguar, although there were double headlights on either side, (as fitted to the road cars in America) rather than the single units seen on the standard British car. For Group A the body shell of the car has to remain untouched in shape and size. The TWR cars were first stripped of all the sound proofing material (which is integral in the standard car) before being fitted with a full roll cage in the otherwise unaltered shell.

Walkinshaw buried the bad memories of Broadspeed at the TT with a fine first-time victory in 1982 (right). Sharing his Motul supported XJ-S with Chuck Nicholson he headed a TWR Jaguar one-two.

In 1983 Jaguar came out and openly supported TWR's two car ETCC title bid. The year got off to a poor start in Italy with Walkinshaw/Nicholson only managing second at Monza and third at Vallelunga (top left) after frustrating delays, but the Big Cat returned to the winner's circle at a misty and damp Donington. The honours went to Brundle/Fitzpatrick/Calderari in car no. seven after the lead car had been badly delayed (above and left).

Lifting spirits on a damp day, the 'works' Jaguars show their prowess at Donington (left and above) in 1983. Nicholson came to a halt due to a lack of petrol — a fuel valve had malfunctioned at the previous stop for replenishment. He had to push the car back to the pits.

As with the Broadspeed cars, the drivers reported that the Jaguar handled remarkably well for such a large car. It was a physical car to drive, but if you were strong enough it had very few vices.

The 60 degree V12 engine was mounted as standard. Walkinshaw's philosophy was to keep the car as simple and as close to the original as possible. The engine regulations made fuel injection an essential pre-requisite due to the restrictions placed on the altering of exhaust manifolds.

In the first season of racing the team en- countered some problems with the hot exhaust melting valve springs when the car was at rest, but this was countered by use of springs from the Cosworth DFV engine. "The problem that was with us all the way," recalls TWR's engine man Alan Scott, "was the underbonnet cooling. On a hot day the engine would lose performance and there would be overheating problems." It was a question of keeping everything as well cooled as possible. The search for the best possible cooling saw the XJ-S sprout various oil coolers at different times in its three year racing history, but it was not really until 1984 that the best solution was found. The first year the two oil coolers were positioned behind the narrow engine grille, for 1983 they dropped down under the bumper becoming almost air scoops. For 1984 however the water radiator was dropped low down in the engine bay leaving plenty of room above for the oil coolers. There was a separate cooling system for the differential and this was an integral part of the Jaguar rear 'spoiler' of 1983.

Within the engine itself, the camshaft profil- ing was changed each year to produce extra horsepower. There was work continuing throughout the project to perfect the best valve shapes to improve the head flow and Cosworth provided special pistons which were redesigned

for the 1984 season. Perhaps most important of all for the car was the fuel injection system.

The first year the XJ-S was fitted with a modified Lucas system as fitted to road Jaguars. This system featured a non-changeable chip, and was replaced for 1983 to allow the system to be reprogrammed. The breakthrough, however, came in 1984. Over the winter of 1983/84 the TWR engine team had its own test bed for the first time and was able to do extensive testing of the engine. The results gave the '84 spec XJ-S much more power through a slight increase in compression ratio, a revised camshaft profile and reprofiled piston crown shapes. The exhaust system, too was altered, with the addition of much larger and longer tail pipes for 1984.

The oil surge problem which had so delayed the Broadspeed project was overcome by TWR early on, after a great deal of development work which produced a complex baffled sump, and an oil 'peeler' on the crank which lifted the oil off the shaft and ducted it away to the sump, thus ensuring that the heat was dissipated efficiently.

Parked forlornly on the outside of Woodcote during the 1983 TT — the Walkinshaw/Nicholson XJ-S after the latter's incident. The Jaguar team was beaten by a TWR Rover on this occasion.

By the start of 1984 the engine had reached the full extent of its development. The engine management system was producing the optimum power. "We simply could not get any more power out of it," comments Walkinshaw, "after that the only extra pace we could find came from tyre developments." The Jaguar had reached its prime, and was winning.

The original XJ-S of 1982 was raced with 16 in. BBS wheels, but later in its career TWR changed to Speedline 17 in. wheels which proved much more efficient for cooling, and at the same time allowed the use of 14 in. AP brake discs. The brakes, however, remained a problem throughout the car's entire career. In the 1984 season, in an effort to overcome overheating at

90

Second victory of 1983 for Walkinshaw/Nicholson. After finding success at the Enna speedbowl the duo went on to win at the fabulous Brno road circuit.

the twistier tracks, the team tried water injected brakes and these proved to be effective. Coming as they did at the end of the Big Cat's European racing career, the development of these units was never carried through to the fullest extent.

Perhaps the most important step in cooling the brakes was the location right from the start, of the rear ventilated discs, outboard rather than inboard as standard. The car featured massive four pot single caliper systems and the outboard location kept the intense heat generated under braking well away from the differential.

The original car was fitted with a standard four speed gearbox but after Spa 1983 this was replaced by a Getrag five speed unit.

The suspension was traditional Jaguar and in keeping with Walkinshaw's philosophy of keeping things simple. The result was a car that was the class of its generation. Although much heavier on fuel consumption than its rivals, due to the extra weight, the speed obtained, thanks to the powerful engine, enabled the drivers to make up enough time to allow themselves time for the stop, and with some very slick pit work from the race mechanics the whole process was kept to the absolute minimum delay.

Such a policy was good for the racing, the extra stop often dropping the cars behind their pursuers, which meant that the Jaguar drivers had to really charge to regain their advantage. The crowds loved it. The Big Cats won a place in their hearts.

In contrast the early days of the Walkinshaw XJ-S had gone almost unnoticed. The motoring press noted in a few meagre paragraphs that Tom Walkinshaw and co-driver Chuck 91

TWR ran three Jaguars in British racing green in 1984. On home soil for the first time, British enthusiasts saw car number two crewed by Percy and Nicholson (previous page) take the laurels. The Walkinshaw/Heyer lead car and third string Schlesser/Calderari entry (above and right) were both delayed, dashing hopes of following up a one-two-three practice order with a similar race outcome — at least on this occasion. But all three cars came home, a testament to TWR's excellent preparation and pit work.

Nicholson had qualified an XJ-S on the front row of the grid for the opening round of the 1982 European Touring Car Championship race at Monza. The car, it was reported, had led the race in convincing fashion until a rough ride over some kerbing had caused a pipe to break, retirement following. That was the story. The car was not a works Jaguar, for it had appeared at the Italian track in black, with sponsorship from Motul and Akai. It was hardly taken seriously. After all, the disaster of the Broadspeed cars had surely put Jaguar off racing for good.

The TWR team, however, was increasingly optimistic. The car raced at Monza had undergone scarcely any testing. Any thoughts that the project was going to be another disaster were dispelled a week later when the drivers took the XJ-S to pole position, fastest race lap and third place at the difficult Vallelunga track in the hills above Rome. People began to take notice. A fortnight later Walkinshaw took the car to its first victory in a round of the Belgian Production Car Championship at Zolder.

In front of a home crowd at Donington Park the car was put out of the race after an early battle for the lead when a stone holed a radiator. Although the team then missed the distant Enna-Pergusa event, it came bouncing back at Mugello, taking pole position at the Florentine circuit. Sharing on this occasion with Belgian Pierre Dieudonne, Walkinshaw again put the car on pole but after a fabulous hour long dice with the BMW 528is and a Chevrolet Camaro, the car retired with engine problems. These were later attributed to the melting of valve springs due to the overheating of the exhaust manifold, and led to the switch to new springs.

Walkinshaw's first international victory came at the fabulous Brno circuit in Czechoslovakia. Back in 1977 the Broadspeed cars had shown that this of all the circuits was one where the V12 would go well and Walkinshaw proved that by dominating the entire weekend. Pole position and a flag to flag victory gave Jaguar its first European long distance race win since the 1960s.

At the Österreichring Walkinshaw once more took pole position, but was delayed during

Joy and heartache for Walkinshaw in 1984. Triumph in the world's most prestigious saloon car race, the Spa 24 Hours (above left) was another stride towards the ETCC crown. Alas, hope of clinching it on home soil at Silverstone (left) was dashed by a blown engine.

the race when a windscreen wiper failed to work properly, which cost more than a lap. Driving the entire race himself, Walkinshaw nonetheless finished second after a memorable charge. To compound his successes he won the next round of the championship at the Nurburgring on BMW home ground, with a pole position time some ten seconds ahead of his nearest rival! People were beginning to sit up and take notice. The Broadspeed cars had been quick, but they had never won, and here was a Scotsman proving it could be done.

The cynics, however, had a field day at Spa. The TWR team was running two cars for the first time, with Walkinshaw and Nicholson being joined by Win Percy and a second car being entered for Pierre Dieudonne, Peter Lovett and Jeff Allam. The race was a disaster. Walkinshaw was on pole again, but this was by now becoming customary. The race in typical Spa weather saw both Jaguars retire after incidents, neither having run well, poor tyres in the wet and mechanical problems holding back their progress.

The team, however, bounced back in style and ended the year with 1-2 finishes, at the Silverstone Tourist Trophy, in front of a home crowd, and at Zolder in Belgium.

The performance of the cars in their first year was such that Egan decided that he would come out and admit to supporting them. At a press conference in London's Dorchester Hotel he announced that 1983 would see a works ETCC team. This move was merely a postscript; it would have been more appropriate to have held the press conference 12 months beforehand.

1983 was to see two green and white Jaguars taking on the revitalised BMW runners, who had high hopes that the new 635CSi would be a match for the XJ-S. Walkinshaw was to be joined in the team by Nicholson, Dieudonne, Swiss Enzo Calderari, experienced saloon campaigners Fitzpatrick and Percy, and an up and coming single seater driver called Martin Brundle, who Walkinshaw had spotted as a real talent in the making.

It was to be a strange year, one marred by

The chequered flag became a familiar sight for the Jaguar drivers in 1984 (below). This is the Donington victory.

Martin Brundle flat out in the XJ-S (above). Walkinshaw spotted his talent long before he graduated to Grand Prix racing with the Tyrrell team in 1984.

protest and controversy. The expectations raised at the end of 1982 survived, but were a little battered. In the course of the year much work was done to improve the car, but it was a disappointment nonetheless. There may have been frustra-

tion, but the team never gave up, despite everything.

The rear axle oil cooler attracted much attention when it first appeared at Monza and was one of several attempts to try to perfect the cooling of the XJ-S. The race, however, was lost by the smallest thing; well ahead of the opposition, Nicholson had to watch as the bonnet of his car began to flap when a clip broke. It was cruel luck indeed. At the flag the Big Cat was just four seconds behind the winning BMW. Vallelunga saw an alarming incident when a wheel collapsed   99

A sudden storm caused chaos during the 1984 TT and cost Walkinshaw/Heyer valuable time. Some stirring driving had all but made up for a cruel delay when the engine blew...

at speed, sending Walkinshaw into a barrier. The other car had been rudely punted out of the race. The Walkinshaw car, however, had limped round and was repaired and it was remarkable that this car went on to record a third place finish. The year, however, had not got off to a good start, and the wheel failure had raised ques-

100

Victory, though remained with the Jaguars as Calderari/Fitzpatrick/Brundle scored a popular win.

Enna-Pergusa saw Walkinshaw and Nicholson finally take the chequered flag, while the second car succumbed to overheating problems. Mugello was spoiled by a plethora of little problems and it was not until the cars got back to the fast sweeps of Brno that things began to look up; Walkinshaw won again, although the second car was delayed by a pit stop for a puncture that never was - a broken rose joint convincing the driver that he had damaged a tyre.

Walkinshaw took victory at the super quick Osterreichring, with Brundle partnering him and the second car of Calderari/Dieudonne 20 seconds behind. At last it looked as if the year was going to improve.

On a blistering hot day at the Nurburgring, both cars failed to make the finish, but Walkinshaw and Nicholson made up for that disappointment by winning in a lone entry at the Salzburgring a week later.

At the prestigious Spa 24 Hours the team once more dominated practice, but with Walkinshaw going out with a clutch problem, it was left to the Brundle/Percy/Calderari car to salvage the honours. In the middle of the night Percy was pushed into a barrier by a backmarker but the seriously delayed car was running till the 17th hour when its gearbox finally gave up.

The Silverstone Tourist Trophy was billed as the BMW versus Jaguar showdown, with the two marques each having taken five wins in the series. That script was upset when a Rover Vitesse gave everyone a surprise - Steve Soper and Rene Metge winning the event, and Walkinshaw had to resort to the second Jag when his car was crashed in the damp by Chuck Nicholson. The second car had started two laps down having overheated when an oil pulley came adrift on the warm up lap.

The championship was to be settled at the final round at Zolder, and in keeping with the tone of the year, it was high drama all the way to the flag with no-one really caring who won as Dieter Quester in his BMW and Win Percy in the Jaguar battled for fourth place. At the flag

tions which needed answering.

Donington Park saw the return to winning form, although Walkinshaw and Nicholson once again were delayed when a fuel valve malfunctioned during the refuelling stop. Nicholson went out without his full fuel load and duly ran out of petrol, having to push his car to the pits.

they were a scant two seconds apart, and the BMW had won. For the Jaguar, it was a case of looking forward to 1984....

The winter months, however, saw intense development of the car at Kidlington and the team went down to Monza for the first race of the season with three cars, by this stage decked out in full British racing green. It was to be a spectacular year in the history of ETCC with the racing close all the way.

At Monza Walkinshaw and his new partner Hans Heyer delivered the challenge to the BMWs, Rovers and Volvos. Further victories followed for the pair at Brno (where Walkinshaw became the first man since Louis Chiron to win the event for a third time), Zeltweg and with Win Percy joining them, in the Spa 24 Hours.

When Walkinshaw and Heyer were not winning Chuck Nicholson and Win Percy made sure that the Jaguar kept its name in the record books, the duo winning at Donington and Salzburgring, while the third car took the flag at Enna-Pergusa with Martin Brundle alongside Enzo Calderari. On two occasions, at Enna and Brno, the team finished 1-2-3. There could be no doubting the fact that the Jaguar had come of age.

Towards the end of the year plans were laid for the cars to be raced in the Far East. At the Macau Grand Prix Walkinshaw led Heyer to a 1-2 victory over the BMWs.

Although it was announced that the Jaguars would not be doing any further ETCC events at the start of 1985, the XJ-S lived on. In June '85 Walkinshaw took one of his beloved Big Cats to Millbrook test track in Bedfordshire and recorded the fastest unofficial time for a saloon car over a single lap - a staggering 174.2 mph. Plans were laid, too, for the cars to be shipped out to the Far East for Macau, Fuji and the James Hardie 1000 classic at Bathurst, Australia.

Why did Walkinshaw succeed where the Broadspeed team failed? Walkinshaw himself believes that the XJ12Cs had the potential to enjoy the same sort of success that fell to the XJ-S. "Those Broadspeed cars should have been winning. As it turned out they went through too long a gestation period. They were always

changing the design of their components and in the end, I think, they ended up at sea. It was a case of rule by committee. For the XJ-S project, I planned out the campaign and then it was passed down to my engineers and middle management and I was able to get on with the driving." A dictatorship it might have been, but something of a benevolent one, and certainly effective.

TWR had a simple approach. As many standard parts as possible were retained; the cars, after all, had been designed after years of research and it was, to Walkinshaw's way of thinking, logical to use the experience of engineers in years past, rather than hunt around for something different.

The XJ-S was the right car at the right time. It fitted the Group A regulations far more than the Broadspeed XJ12C ever did Group Two. The relationship between TWR and the Jaguar factory, too, was an object lesson. While the Broadspeed men had been publicly linked to Coventry and had suffered at the hands of the factory in terms of parts, TWR was almost clandestine in its relationship with the factory, but the back up it received was substantial.

There is no doubt that Walkinshaw and Egan hit it off right from the start - they were like-minded men. There was a job to do and both wanted to do it, and get it right. Walkinshaw laid out what he wanted from the factory and Egan made sure he got it. When success came Egan and his men in sales and marketing were able to reap the rewards in advertising. Walkinshaw himself credits Egan with much of the success, "It was he who got the whole project going, and from there it snowballed; everyone in the company was behind the project."

Although the TWR Jaguars did not dominate totally until their third season in racing, success was slowed down early on by small problems: a loose bonnet, a sticking fuel valve. In motor racing it is easy to blame luck for failures, but in 1983 in particular, the Jaguars did suffer more than their fair share of misfortune.

The secret of the project, however, was its constant momentum, the fine tuning and refining of the car until all the problems were solved. There were none of the wholesale changes of the Broadspeed days, but rather tweaks here and there. The oil surge was cured early on, by a complex system of baffles in the oil sump. There was no need to cry for dry sumping, which was contrary to the regulations. The cooling system took the longest to sort out, but once that was developed the car was on its way to success.

A great deal of credit has to go to Alan Scott and his engineers at TWR; they squeezed more and more power from the V12 until in the end they reached the end of the possible development within the confines of Group A.

Walkinshaw and his team thrive on success. Once the XJ-S had fulfilled its potential they began to look ahead again - and so was born the Jaguar XJR-6 Group C project.

Just a touch of oversteer ... the 1984 XJ-S wasn't an easy car to drive and it took a firm hand to master it. Note the angle of the inside front wheel.

JAGUAR V12

The I.M.S.A. Prototype

When the TR8s of Bill Adam and Bob Tullius finished 1-2 in the GTO class at IMSA's 1980 Daytona finale it was the end of the road for the Triumph programme - and, on the face of it, for the Group 44 racing team. MG had gone and the Triumph and Rover cars were being dropped in the States. Only Jaguar remained, and it was losing £1 million a week. After twenty years association with the Leyland marques' it looked as though it was all over for Tullius.

Irrepressible, while sadly laying off most of his staff, Tullius was putting a very ambitious plan to the sick Jaguar company. His hope, and indeed the very hopes of salvation for the marque itself, lay in Jaguar's newly granted independence. Tullius suggested to the new board, headed by the optimistic Egan, a return to tradition. He suggested a recovery go hand in hand with a return to Le Mans.

Tullius had seen the potential in the new IMSA GTP regulations for a prototype powered by the Jaguar V12 engine. After two years of GTO racing, overshadowed by the faster GTX cars, he was ready to move up to the big league - and the new GTP class, to run with GTX, gave him, on paper, the chance to do so in conjunction with Jaguar. It also opened the way for a Le Mans bid, a new prototype era dawning for the French classic.

The seventies had witnessed a decline in the strength and prestige of the world's greatest endurance race. It was dragged down by the sickness of World Championship sports car racing which, under Group Five silhouette regulations, degenerated into a series of events contested by Porsche 935 equipped privateers. True, Le Mans had opted out of the World Championship altogether and had been rewarded by some superb battles between Porsche and Renault Group Six sports-racers over the years 1976-78, but after Renault had achieved its goal and withdrawn to concentrate upon Grand Prix racing, the Group Six days were effectively over and Group Five offered precious little in its place.

The Le Mans organisers devised their own 'GTP' class for fully enclosed sports-racing prototypes and the concept was seized on by IMSA, which was also faced with a procession of Porsche 935s. By 1980 the FIA had announced that the World Championship would be switched to GTP-style Group C cars, so Jean Rondeau's victory at Le Mans that year in a prototype of his own design and construction marked the beginning of a new age.

IMSA President John Bishop's version of GTP was based around a formula that specified minimum weight according to engine type - for example, a car powered by a three litre, four valves per cylinder racing engine would have to weigh at least 900 kg, while a car carrying a two litre four valve per cylinder turbocharged engine

would need to register a minimum of 1000kg.

A two valves per cylinder stock block engine like the Jaguar V12, with a capacity of up to 6.0 litres, would have to weigh no less than 900 kg. With turbocharged power plants restricted to 3.4 litres, and at that capacity two valves per cylinder, even in the heaviest, 1000 kg division, the Coventry V12's potential looked good, even at 700 cc short of the minimum permissible displacement for the 900 kg division.

Tullius' plan for an IMSA GTP car with long term Le Mans potential aroused excitement within the re-structured, more autonomous Jaguar organisation. Mike Dale, still heading the marketing side of Jaguar Cars Inc., calculated that to keep Group 44 going as a racing team would mean selling 200 more Jaguars a year in the USA. Typifying the new spirit that had entered the marque, he resolved to find a way.

Dale's philosophy was that to undertake something as ambitious as a GTP programme would play down the company's problems and suggest to the rest of the world that things were - well, better than they really were at that time. It would also provide a focus for the renewed optimism that came with the release of Jaguar Cars Ltd from the centralizing forces of Leyland.

The new Jaguar management team under Egan didn't take long to approve the concept. Two of Egan's primary concerns were presenting the best possible image for the company and carrying on its traditions. A prototype programme would do both. Tullius got his plan approved, and his reprieve for 1981. After a year of Trans Am racing while the prototype was at the design stage, he could reflect;"I'd got to the stage of disbanding the Group 44 as a racing team, then the effect of John Egan's arrival at Coventry began to be reflected over here. I'd worked with Mike Dale for years - he was quite a

Lee Dykstra penned the XJR-5's distinctive shape with reference to the results of numerous wind tunnel runs using one quarter scale models (left). This is the most highly developed pre-construction model. The wind tunnel programme continued throughout the life of the car, aerodynamics playing a vital role in its development.

racer himself in SCCA - and he knew our capabilities. We were given some rope in 1981 and we didn't hang ourselves. We'd begun to do well again and so had Jaguar; from these factors came acceptance of the GTP project".

Jaguar played down its involvement in the 1981 design phase of the GTP car, but funded it entirely, and as the car began to take shape in 1982 it was ready to announce a GTP race programme for Group 44. Dale justified the U.S. operation's financial support for the project by comparing the cost with prime time TV advertising and by pointing to its role in helping build an image, "increasing the perceived value of our cars".

In addition to Jaguar's wholehearted support, Tullius continued to receive backing from Quaker State oil and Goodyear. Indeed, he had now bought a Quaker State distributorship in Winchester, Virginia and early in 1982 he moved Group 44 from its long standing Dulles Airport base to land adjoining the oil business, not far from the team's birthplace, at Falls Church.

For Tullius, 1982 was lined up as a learning year, after two decades of production racing. "Racing victories and title chances will come, this is just the start of a multi-year effort", he explained.

By 1982 the GTP class was established in the IMSA Camel GT series, although the first cars, from March and Lola, had only appeared the previous year. March built a BMW powered and backed contender, Lola a Chevrolet engined rival. The March M1/C-BMW ushered in the GTP era at Riverside in April 1981, but the car was not a success. In contrast, the Lola-Chevrolet, on static display at the same meeting, took to the track one week later at Laguna Seca, also in California, and was an instant winner. Expatriate Englishman Brian Redman was the driving force behind, and in the cockpit of, the Lola T600 and he went on to win the 1981 IMSA crown, overthrowing the reign of the 935 Group 5/GTX car, and doing wonders for Lola's order books.

That wasn't the end of the 935, however, for as 1982 unfolded the 935 was still numerically superior by far. Redman hadn't dominated 107

The structural elements of the XJR-5 are laid bare. Note how the long engine block is used as a stressed member, with the rear suspension hung from the transaxle. The long nosebox, behind-front-wheel-axis pedal location, steel tube roll cage and tubular re-inforced cockpit bulkheads afford good protection for the driver.

Jaguar V12 Race Cars

Clean lines of the XJR-5 as it was presented in public in the summer of 1982. The shape would outwardly alter little over the next three years but underneath the car many important changes were wrought as the team adapted the ground effect under body to suit different circuits and conditions.

meetings with the Lola and rendered it obsolete. He had often been outqualified by the better driven 935s, and outrun in the early stages. However, he would pick off the more powerful Porsches as they dropped back to normal race boost.

Even at race boost the 935 offered in excess

of 700 bhp, whereas Redman's normally aspirated Chevrolet was producing less than 600 bhp. The Lola scored on grip, handling and manoeuvrability. Eric Broadley's T600 design had a thoroughbred, no compromise ground effect monocoque chassis. The 935 was, for all its radical Group 5/GTX modifications, a produc-

tion car at heart, with its flat six engine hung out behind the rear axle.

Powered by a mighty four valves per cylinder, 3.2 litre turbocharged engine, the K3 version of the 935 developed by the Kremer brothers in Cologne was a complicated and expensive motor car. The Lola-Chevrolet offered a simpler alternative at half the price.

In theory, Tullius could have developed a GTX Jaguar from the Trans Am car, but it would have needed a long and expensive turbocharging programme to have matched Porsche power. And with prototypes coming back, it would have had poor long term prospects. On the other hand, an IMSA GTP car had excellent future Le Mans prospects, the race returning to the World Championship, which kept its doors opened to all engines, thanks to the instigation of a fuel consumption formula. As with IMSA, the Group C rulemakers were seeking 800/900 kg cars with 600/650 bhp on tap. A Jaguar V12 powered prototype promised to fit the bill.

Whereas the Trans Am series concentrated on sprint racing, IMSA's Camel GT series incorporated a number of World Championship style endurance races, highlighted by Daytona's 24 Hour classic. This was the race used to warm the team up in early 1982, following an approach by Goodyear, which wanted to put the Trans Am XJ-S onto street radials. As previously related, it was an outing bugged by gearbox problems - the forthcoming prototype would have a Hewland VG5-200 race box rather than the standard Jaguar unit. The six Weber equipped Group 44 V12 was now producing in the region of 570 bhp.

Running at 6900 rpm in the interests of reliability (and geared for 190 mph), the V12 tended by Fuerstenau (on a freelance basis these days) and in-house engine man John Huber, sang sweetly throughout the Daytona 24 Hour marathon. For the GTP programme there would, initially, only be slight modifications to cylinder heads, and ancillary equipment. The power would be transmitted through a three plate Borg and Beck clutch to a commonplace Hewland long distance racing gearbox to ensure

111

a dependable power train. In over 100 practice, qualifying and racing outings since 1974 the V12 only suffered a handful of failures.

For the design of the chassis Tullius had turned, early in 1981, to top American road racing designer Lee Dykstra's Grand Rapids, Michigan based freelance agency, 'Special Chassis Inc.'. In February of that year he had asked Dykstra to submit a design and cost proposal for a GTP car with 24 hour and specifically Le Mans potential and terms had been quickly agreed. The rest of the year had been taken up by Dykstra's careful design work, which embraced numerous wind tunnel investigations.

For Dykstra, the project was in some respects, a logical extension of an existing Can Am programme. His CRC Chemicals backed design, constructed and driven by Al Holbert, was one of the more successful home-grown cars in American road racing.

Dykstra had a long experience of road racing, having built SCCA racers at night when he first graduated from college with a degree in mechanical engineering, taking a day job with Cadillac. He was eventually spotted by Ford's competition wing and enjoyed a successful relationship with the company working on the GT40 and later Trans Am cars. When Ford's racing activities were curtailed in the Seventies he moved over to 'safety cars'.

Dykstra began his association with Holbert in the mid Seventies, developing a Chevrolet Monza for IMSA racing. In 1979 the pair worked together on a spaceframe Can Am car powered by the ubiquitous Chevrolet V8 engine. The car was commissioned by Carl Hogan and backed by Busch beer - it was called the Hogan Racing HR001 'Buschmobile'. In fact, the original plan had been to develop a Lola, but the converted car was burned out in a pre-season testing accident so the replacement was called for rather late in the day. Worse, the team was under-financed and Holbert got fed up and quit before the end of the season.

Holbert's partnership with Dykstra flourished once again in 1980 when he branched out with his own CRC sponsored team. Dykstra produced the CAC-1 for it - a neat, straightfor-

ward ground effect car in best Formula One practice. It employed a narrow monocoque with integral fuel tank between the cockpit and stressed drivetrain leaving plenty of space for long, wide venturi tunnels either side of it. The tunnels were sealed by sliding skirts.

Constructed by Holbert's Warrington, Pennsylvania team, the CAC-1-Chevrolet became the first all-American car to win Can Am honours since the Chaparral days of the late Sixties. Holbert took two victories and finished second overall in the standings to Carl Haas' ever-dominant Lola-Chevrolet. To get to grips with the Haas Lola in 1981, Dykstra designed a smaller, sleeker, lighter car, dubbed the CRC-2, which proved very fast on the straight and won three races. This car was the point of reference for Group 44's prototype, which Dale dubbed XJR-5.

IMSA GTP regulations demand that the driver's feet be located behind the axis of the front wheels for safety reasons. Conventional ground effect cars, having a single, central fuel tank rather than the traditional pannier tanks either side of the driver, tend to place the driver's feet ahead of the front wheel axis, due to the combined length of the driver cell, tank and drivetrain. Keeping the feet behind the axis necessitates a long wheelbase - that of the XJR-5 is 108.5 in. The wheelbase of contemporary Porsche 956 ground effects car, comforming only to Group C as it put the driver's feet ahead of the front wheel axis, was 102.5 in.

Dykstra reports no drawback from the long wheelbase. The XJR-5's central tank, on the other hand, leaves room for ground effect venturis, assists the rigidity of the monocoque and ensures a constant weight distribution, regardless of fuel load. It also keeps the car Group C legal, which was a major consideration in view of the Le Mans aspirations. Needing a car legal for both IMSA and Group C, Group

In 1983 car 44's main rival on the IMSA trail was the Al Holbert run and driven March 83G-Porsche (right). Car 14's turbo power gave it the edge over the Jaguar at most circuits, cockpit boost control aiding Holbert's title winning effort.

44's prototype had to feature a flat bottom area of 800 mm x 1000 mm between the front and rear wheels. This reduced the plan area available for venturi tunnels. Neither regulating body allowed sliding skirts.

Three separate sessions in the University of Michigan's one-quarter scale wind tunnel and a total of 157 test runs with a model so detailed it even simulated the suspension and radiator impact on the air flow, came between the starting point, a roofed CRC-2 shape, and the final, distinctive XJR-5 lines. Compared with the

original Can Am spyder, there was a much greater emphasis on drag reduction, an essential consideration with a view to Daytona's banking and the three mile Mulsanne straight at Le Mans. The CRC-2 was all about ground effect, but in view of the need for a two seater cockpit and the flat bottom/no skirt regulations, there was no way that a prototype could hope to achieve the same level of downforce.

Dykstra's design incorporated ground effect tunnels running from behind the flat bottom area alongside the long engine block, curving upwards towards the rear to exit under the rear wing. The wing helps extract the air from the tunnels and acts as a 'trim tab'. The ground effect is produced in the front, shallow part of the venturis but clean extraction of air is important in maximising the effectiveness of the underbody aerodynamics. The XJR-5's distinctive twin tail booms are significant in that IMSA regulations dictate that a rear wing may not extend outside the body plan.

The over and under body shapes have to be considered as a whole, for both interact to produce the overall aerodynamic package. Of crucial importance is how air enters the venturis as well as how it is extracted, and, of course, how the air that is not diverted under the car flows over it.

Dykstra aimed "to design a machine capable of 200 mph given the V12's power, with a favourable lift/drag ratio and good pitch balance". The lift/drag ratio is the ratio between the amount of negative lift generated by the car - which is up to twice its own weight in the case of a prototype, but varies with speed - and the aerodynamic drag, which can also be measured in pounds, and of course, influences top speed. The plus-200 mph speed attained by the XJR-5 at Daytona and Le Mans and its excellent track behaviour suggest that Dykstra got his sums right.

Underneath the carefully shaped skin of the Jaguar prototype is a monocoque chassis with an aluminium honeycomb floor, tubular re-inforced steel bulkheads, integral fuel tank with up to 120 litre capacity and a built-in mandatory steel roll cage. The engine is fully stressed. The suspen-

sion follows conventional racing practice with upper and lower wishbones, Koni spring/-damper units and anti-roll bars at each end, and was inherited from the CRC-2. At the rear the spring/damper units are mounted high, above the upper wishbone, to clear the venturi tunnels.

The brakes were positioned outboard - four pot single calipers acting on cast iron ventilated discs - the brake layout also inherited from the Can Am car. Lockheed supplied the braking equipment, Jongbloed the 15 in. diameter modular wheels - 11½ in. wide at the front, 14 in. wide at the rear. The XJR-5 was in the GTP mainstream in its inevitable use of Group 44 backer Goodyear's tyres.

Engine installation proved a major headache for Dykstra, the V12 representing a major departure from the usual V8 lump. In particular, the length and the centre of gravity of the Chevrelot and Jaguar engines differ considerably. From the point of view of cooling, putting the radiators in the nose is theoretically the most efficient solution. However Dykstra stuck with a CRC-2 type side mounted layout, which is better from the point of view of weight distribution and minimises pipe runs. The airflow is diverted either side of the cockpit, down into the radiator then back up onto the rear deck. The water radiator sits in the left pod, an oil radiator in the right one.

From Dykstra's painstaking design, the XJR-5 was constructed by Group 44 over the period June 1981 to May 1982. The car was officially announced by Jaguar on 7 January 1982 and at that stage a début at Sebring in March was considered likely. However, the job was not rushed; the car was built carefully and well and was not ready to run until the summer. Tullius' team took full advantage of being able to prepare the contender away from the pressure of a championship programme.

The 5.3 litre prototype first ran at Summit Point in June and in late July Jaguar's engineering chief Jim Randle flew out to see it in action at Road America, following further runs at Road Atlanta. Tullius and Adam ran a simulated race under the gaze of the Coventry man on the four mile long Wisconsin circuit and couldn't find a major fault with the car. Randle returned to base highly impressed. Group 44 was becoming a semi-works effort and Heynes and Hassan's successor was able to report that (Group 44) "are a great bunch ... so adaptable and so very competent, and a credit to the name of Jaguar; to reach such a standard, this quickly, really is an achievement".

John Egan went to witness the car's race début for himself. It came at the same circuit in late August. The car finished a highly creditable third. "Who could ask for more?", remarked the Jaguar chief.

An unfortunate crash practicing for the next Camel GT event at Mid Ohio in early September did not ruffle Tullius. "1982 is a development year", he reminded critics, "everything we do with the XJR-5, right through Daytona's three hour finale, is calculated to make us 100% ready for 1983. That's when you'll see us in the hunt".

Refettled, with a number of modifications, including lighter body panels, the car appeared in the two season closing Camel events. Sadly the V12 swallowed something it didn't like at Pocono and became one of a number of flat tyre victims at Daytona. The newcomer was both unlucky and overweight. Nevertheless, on the basis of its 1982 form *Automobile Sport* was moved to remark that 'the car is a potential winner in 1983 long distance races, despite the handicap of an engine that is 100 bhp down on a Chevrolet and nearly 300 bhp down from a 935'.

Both the Lola-Chevrolet and the 935 had been used by 1982 champion John Paul Junior. The young American charger's JPR team had built its own spaceframe 935s, first the JLP-3, then the more radical JLP-4 with pure racing suspension, designed by none other than Lee Dykstra.

Dykstra's preoccupation, however, in 1983 was the development of the XJR-5, which faced a long gruelling season from the Daytona 24 Hours in February to the Daytona 3 Hours in November. Indeed, the car would run the best part of three full seasons before it was replaced. Over that period it underwent a major transformation, such that by the summer of '85, just

prior to the scheduled introduction of the replacement XJR-7, Dykstra could report that "99.9%" of the components of the original car had been redrawn. Weight saving and aerodynamic development were major concerns, in addition to the never ending quest for greater reliability. For example, the gearbox benefited from better cooling, an easier shift and longer gear life. Group 44 developed its own sideplates to provide a stiffer ring gear support.

In terms of weight, Dykstra reckoned to save a total of 200 lb. getting closer to the weight limit, if not right on it. The final step had to be the lightweight composite monocoque of the XJR-7.

In the refinement of the aerodynamics, and the continual adaption to suit differing circuits, Dykstra reckons to have made around 500 wind tunnel runs, using both the Williams Grand Prix team's rolling road and the large Lockheed full sized facility, in Britain and the States, respectively. He developed a number of different packages suiting different circuit characteristics, including, for example, a choice of five different nose shapes. The bodywork material was switched to a carbon/Kevlar composite as part of the diet programme.

The most fundamental change to the chassis came over the winter of 1984/85, when Dykstra introduced elements of the XJR-7 design, including a revised bellhousing, gearbox and underbody. By 1985 the car was running on bigger 16 in. BBS wheels, 12 in. wide at the front.

The engine was continually improved, the biggest step being an increase to the full permissible 6.0 litre capacity. The bigger capacity unit was developed by Group 44 working with Fuerstenau. It was introduced for 1984, along with a Lucas Micos engine management system. Coventry hired Lucas to develop a Micos electronically managed fuel injection/ignition system. Initially this provided better throttle response and over time it allowed the fuel consumption to be improved and also opened up the way to intake and exhaust modifications which provided more power and more torque. By 1985 the unit had been developed, with technical back up from Coventry, to produce around 650 bhp. 115

Jaguar V12 Race Cars

Indeed, between 1981 and 1985, under the less stringent regulations of GTP, Group 44 had found an extra 100 bhp and 100 lb./ft torque, the best engine of the nine in the '85 batch producing a hefty 670 bhp. The power increase was down to three factors: the increased capacity, work on the flow characteristics of the heads and the intake and exhaust improvements allowed by the Micos system.

Between 1983 and 1985 chassis and engine improvements were such that the XJR-5's Mid Ohio lap time was reduced from 1 min. 27.5 sec. to 1 min 21.8 sec., using similar tyres.

Group 44 had become entirely sponsored by Jaguar in 1983, after twenty years of carrying Quaker State colours. That was the year in which Coventry announced its official backing for the Walkinshaw ETCC effort. Jaguar was in

racing in a way that it hadn't been since the early Sixties.

The biggest threat to Tullius' 1983 title aspirations came, ironically enough, from Al Holbert in a car sponsored by CRC Chemicals - but not one designed by Dykstra. Holbert equipped himself with a March 83G, a chassis developed by the British race car manufacturer from the aftermath of the ill-fated M1/C project,

and suitable for a variety of power plants. The standard option was the good old Chevrolet V8

The XJR-5 showed immense promise at the new Miami Grand Prix in 1983 , before the race was washed out. In 1984 the team went back to win.

but March was keen to exploit the Porsche turbo engine and, with the support of Stuttgart, Holbert's was the works development car. Porsche didn't yet produce an IMSA legal version of its 956, so it was keen to co-operate with March and Holbert's American tuner, Alvin Springer.

Springer's California based Andial concern built the best Porsche engines in IMSA. They were usually 3.2 litre GTX units with water-cooled four valve per cylinder heads and twin turbos, but for GTP only an old style air cooled two valve head and a single turbo set up was legal. Nevertheless, well over 600 bhp was produced by the 934 type, 3.1 litre Andial GTP engine. Neither the Chevrolet V8 (which Holbert used on occasions before the Porsche chassis was ready) nor the Jaguar V12 could ap-

proach that, but the unblown units offered greater torque, for 1983 running in the same 900 kg division.

Notwithstanding the fact that both in 1981 and 1982 the Lola-Chevrolet had more often than not been the car to beat, there was little in the way of strong Lola representation in 1983. John Paul Junior switched to Indy Car racing and two of his leading challengers, Danny Ongias and Ted Field disappeared with the sudden retirement of Field's Interscope Lola team during the second round.

Early in the season the powerful John Fitzpatrick Racing team (which won the 1980 Camel GT series) ran a 935 but that organisation's future lay in World Endurance Championship racing with a Porsche 956 and its early departure to Europe left the 935 challenge wanting.

Anyhow, the old warhorse was gradually becoming outmoded as the GTP field strengthened.

Ford made a factory effort in the 1983 Camel series, at first running a Group Five Zakspeed spaceframe Capri with the appropriate American Mustang bodyshell. This German sprint race special with its 1.7 litre four valve/cylinder turbo engine was replaced mid way through the season by a high-tech, ground effect, but still front-engined Mustang GTP car, with composite monocoque and 2.1 litre motor rated at over 700 bhp. The theory went that the front engine placement allowed plenty of space for ground effect tunnels. The device was certainly quick, but it lacked reliability.

Fast and reliable, the March 83G-Porsche, when it eventually arrived in mid season, was the class of '83. The XJR-5 was its closest challenger.

The traditional 24 hour season opener saw a three driver line up for car no. 44, Tullius and regular partner Adam (a Canadian in his mid thirties with a long Chevrolet powered road racing career behind him) joined by American journalist-cum-racer Pat Bedard. On this occasion the opposition consisted primarily of a fleet of rugged 935s, which could turn up the boost

Brian Redman teamed with Hurley Haywood for the latter races of 1984 and the Anglo-American driving partnership, which extended into 1985, worked well. The ex-Porsche aces found it of great mutual benefit.

Jaguar V12 Race Cars

for qualifying. The Jaguar was kept back to the fourth row, but Tullius proved capable of running with the leaders in the early stages and even had a brief moment of glory between laps five and seven.

A 935 shared by Holbert, Hurley Haywood and Bruce Leven became the pace-setter, only to hit turbo trouble at nightfall. Alas, Group 44 could not profit, the screaming Jaguar delayed by a broken right front wheelbearing. This later caused suspension failure. The race was won by Preston Henn/Bob Wollek/Claude Ballot-Lena/A. J. Foyt's 935.

From Daytona the Camel trail went down the coast to Miami for a new street race that was washed out and abandoned after only 27 treacherous laps. Driving magnificently, Tullius had hauled the Big Cat up from 11th on the grid to fifth place when the premature chequered flag announced Holbert's March-Chevrolet as the victor.

At the much faster Sebring airfield circuit three weeks later the Jaguar was once again an early leader, Tullius and Adam looking very strong. Alas, a blown head gasket left the 12 hours as yet another 935 dominated marathon, Leven's third placed example again shared with Holbert who consequently headed the points table as the series moved to Georgia. Holbert, however, was invited to drive a works Porsche 956 in the Monza 1000 km World Endurance Championship race and was therefore absent on the occasion of the XJR-5's first triumph. It wasn't the fastest car at the fourth round of the series on the Road Atlanta circuit but as the pick of the opposition wilted, Tullius/Adam moved ahead. Before half the scheduled 500 km had been completed, the Jaguar was in command.

From joy to heartache. Having crossed the continent to Riverside, California, the green and white contender hit oil and spun into an ungainly retirement. In contrast, Holbert's March-Chevrolet finished runner up to Fitzpatrick's 935, and the points leader went on to win the May Day 100 mile sprint at Laguna Seca the following weekend. Tullius found more luck on his second Californian outing, collecting second after Bobby Rahal's spaceframe Mustang had

been penalized for a jumped start.

From California, Holbert flew back to Europe, this time to test the brand new 83G-Porsche at Goodwood in England. The car proved satisfactory and was promptly dispatched to the States. Four days after clearing customs it took the chequered flag first on Charlotte, North Carolina's combined banked oval and road

Brian Redman (above) made an unexpected return to racing in 1984 (right) to chase that elusive Le Mans win. The 1981 IMSA champion had won almost every other sportscar classic during his long career. He quickly found success in Ralph Sanchez' 'instant-classic' Miami Grand Prix.

course. The XJR-5 had encouragingly shared the front row with the new contender and Tullius even led the first lap. Then Holbert went through and shortly afterwards the Jaguar hit accident debris, which cost a stop for a new nose. That, mind you, wasn't the end of the Coventry challenge. Tullius and Adam strove mightily to regain ground and soon after one third distance in the 500 km race repassed the March, which was conserving an overheating engine. The Jaguar led until almost half distance, then a tyre deflated while it was on the banking, causing contact with the wall. Third place was salvaged.

Jaguar V12 Race Cars

The sweeping Lime Rock Park circuit saw the March-Porsche again outrun the Jaguar, at the end of May. However, in the second of two three-hour heats it was struck by a turbo problem. Adam brushed a slower car in the same heat, requiring a new nose cone, but that didn't stop the second win of the season. The XJR-5 was the only car to go 174 laps on aggregate.

With eight of 17 rounds now run, Holbert's impressive points tally was 106 but Tullius and Adam were strongly placed in second and third, on 75 and 52, respectively. The weekend of 18/19 June brought no change in the points situation, but more heartache for Tullius and more happiness for Holbert. The former crashed out of a wet Mid Ohio six hour race due to a misunderstanding with a backmarker, while the latter won Le Mans with the works Porsche team.

Holbert was back for the Daytona night race, only to retire, as did the XJR-5. However, he finally did increase his points lead the following weekend at Brainerd, where the Jaguar's game pursuit of him ended in another head gasket failure.

Car 44 got into the lead once more at Sears Point, taking command as the March-Porsche made its first fuel stop. Victory looked within grasp when a bolt sheared in the rear suspension, pitching Tullius into the guard rail. Holbert's sixth win gave him the Camel title.

Ironically, Tullius/Adam won two of the remaining five races of the season, while Holbert won only the Daytona finale. The Group 44 victories came at Mosport, where the Big Cat was on pole before running away with the 6 hour race while Holbert lost time repairing a broken exhaust, and at Pocono where there was another splendid pole position plus race success, this time over 500 miles and after Holbert had suffered fuel injection maladies.

Right to the end of the season the turbo car had an edge, but Group 44 had the 6.0 litre engine and Micos system ready for 1984. With more power and better fuel economy, the team expanded to a two car operation, Brian Redman announcing the third comeback of a long and distinguished career to take a lead role in car 04.

The 46 year old Jacksonville, Florida based driver, who had won every sports car classic of note apart from Le Mans, announced his decision in December 1983 and immediately began testing a 6.0 litre Micos equipped car at Daytona.

Conceived in August, the fuel efficient, big capacity unit had first been bench tested the previous month. It was initially to be used in one of the two cars, while the other had a standard 6.0 litre engine. In 04 Redman's partner would be either Bedard or American sports car regular Doc Bundy, Adam having switched to the Ford camp.

In 1984, with the help of the Micos gadgetry, Group 44 would make its first, ambitious Le Mans bid. This cost a number of Camel Championship events. On the domestic scene the chief opposition came not from March-Porsche, but from a new all-Porsche GTP car, the 962. Holbert turned the March over to the Kreepy Krauly team and switched his attention to the new Stuttgart challenger, running a works-backed effort.

The 962 was simply a lengthened wheelbase version of the all-conquering European 956, with the pedals thereby brought behind the front wheel axis. As the 956 weighed in at less than 850 kg, Porsche opted to ballest the 962 to 850 kg and run a 2.8 litre version of the two valve IMSA engine. The works development car was run in the Daytona 24 Hour race by the factory where it proved fast but fragile but thereafter the effort was left to Holbert and a number of privateers. The patient customers lost the first third of the season in late delivery of the cars, then discovered that the 2.8 motor lacked sufficient torque to deal with the surprise of '84, the 'Blue Thunder' team of March-Chevrolets. It wasn't until Springer had supplied replacement 3.2 litre engines (and the cars had been ballasted accordingly to 900 kg) that the new Porsche became a regular race winner.

Springer's bigger engine (100 cc larger than that used by Holbert in '83, thanks to continuing development work) maintained a healthy advantage of Stuttgart horses over Coventry's 6.0 litre best. The German cars raced with over 650 bhp

Doc Bundy was the highest scoring Jaguar driver prior to
the 1984 Daytona finale. A crash cost him his chance of a
top five points position and for 1985 the 1984 Miami co-
victor switched to the Ford camp.

(as much as the more powerful but fuel
restricted four valve 956s in the World Endurance Championship), while the Jaguars enjoyed little more than 610 bhp. And the time and
resource consuming Le Mans bid, which cost
three race appearances, knocked Tullius' title
hopes for six.

Blue Thunder was present throughout the
period before the Porsches got up to speed and,
using 650 bhp Chevrolet V8 propelled March
84Gs, took the initiative in the points race. Not
even a strong late charge by Holbert and partner

Derek Bell could stop the team's surprise high
scorer Randy Lanier scooping the crown. The
5.7 litre VDS engined Blue Thunder cars tended
by ex-March engineer Keith Leighton weren't
the most sophisticated machines on the grid, nor
was Lanier the fastest driver (although teammate
Bill Whittington could hold his own in Indy Car
racing), but the March-Chevrolet package was
good and solid, and so was the cockpit work.

In retrospect, the Group 44 effort could
equally well have profited from the long delay in
962 competitiveness. Indeed, the Virginia team
was heading the points chart when it first missed
an event through the priority afforded to the Le
Mans outing. The team doesn't regret its decision, though. Le Mans glory was and, at the
time of writing still is, the ultimate target for the
GTP programme.   123

Jaguar V12 Race Cars

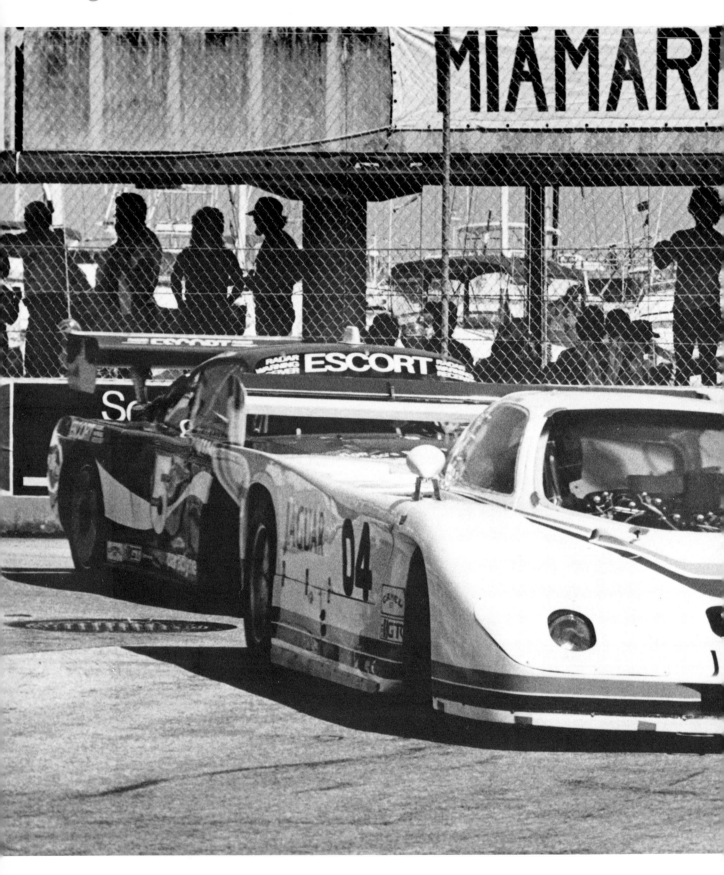

The I.M.S.A. Prototype

In 1984 the Daytona 24 Hour race was a warm up for Le Mans, as much as the start of the IMSA season. It saw an impressive line up in the Jaguar encampment, with three of the six chassis built for the year on show. As usual, there would be three drivers to a car, English veteran David Hobbs joining the crew of 44, Californian veteran Jim Adams helping out with 04. Adams put Redman's Micos engined machine sixth on the grid while Tullius wound up an excellent third fastest, headed only by the Kreepy Krauly liveried March and the factory 962. The front row occupants led the opening laps but the Jaguars could run 15 minutes longer between stops, which put 44 in front while 04 stopped for repairs to a broken nose frame, losing a total of 45 minutes.

As evening came the 962, the swiftest runner in the race, hit transmission trouble, leaving 44 and its old rival to contest the lead. Tullius and co. led 101 laps, looking very strong, until, mid evening, the Jaguar came in with a broken alternator belt. This problem had shown up in long distance trials during December's Daytona testing and the team was at work on a revised system. In the meantime it had only a makeshift solution. Three more such breakages handed the race to the Kreepy Krauly team, the final breakage costing all hope of second place. Car 44 collected third, 28 laps behind the winner. However, 04 was in deeper trouble, having lost an additional two hours with a broken water pump pulley to finish a lowly 24th. Redman at least had the satisfaction of fastest lap, and expressed himself enthusiastic about his chances with the ultra-professional Winchester operation.

That enthusiasm looked well placed after the second round; the Miami street race. The Jaguar challenge was again off the qualifying

The 1984 XJR-5 in street fighting mode. Note the solitary, limited headlight opening to assist a rapid passage through the Miami traffic and the two tier rear wing. Pictured overleaf is the improved 1985 XJR-5 with revised rear end and more powerful engine which made its debut at Daytona. Note the rear wing and tail end treatment for the fast Florida circuit compared with the set up for the nearby slow Miami venue evident on this page.

125

pace, but Redman burst through from the second row to lead into the first corner and hold command for the first 28 of the scheduled 118 laps before Klaus Ludwig's hi-tech Mustang took over. The Mustang, however, had rooted its tyres.

Two laps later Redman was back in command. Meanwhile, Tullius was moving up steadily and he took over the lead when Redman made his scheduled stop on lap 53. By the time both XJR-5s had pitted Bundy in 04 was in the lead and his only problem was a quick spin while trying to lap Bedard. In the end car 44 finished 81 seconds in arrears, the only other car on the same lap. The Jaguars had run the three hours of America's richest sports car race on one fuel stop.

Fired by his magnificent triumph, Redman, sharing once again with Bedard, put 04 on pole for Florida's third IMSA event, at Sebring, and led the first lap. Tullius then took over to head the early stages, fending off the Kreepy Krauly March until the ex-Holbert car suffered an engine malady. Tullius/Bundy commanded the first quarter of the marathon, then a puncture upset the demonstration, followed by a recurrence of the alternator drive belt problem. Later a drivetrain overhaul put 44 right out of contention and finally a fuel system malady spelt retirement. This weekend 04 ran without the Micos system but it lost 33 laps with an ignition fault and rear suspension problem. Redman, however, had the satisfaction of another fastest lap in regaining a total of four laps on the leaders in the late stages.

From Florida the series moved, as usual, to Road Atlanta, the circuit owned by Bill and Don Whittington of the Blue Thunder team - and who scored a rousing one - two success to back up a good second place (to an old 935) at Sebring. Redman/Bedard were the best-of-the-rest in Georgia, finishing the 500 km one lap down,

Daytona debut for Tullius' 1985 challenger — sadly the team boss crashed out of the race in a fiery accident. Tyre deflation was blamed for the incident, which left Tullius with minor burns. Overleaf the car is pictured lapping one of the many slower runners that can delay progress around the combined oval and road course.

while an incident which befell Bundy dropped 44 to 33rd.

IMSA moved on to California without Group 44 this year, thanks to a Le Mans test run. In the team's absence, the 962 made its first appearance as customer car at Riverside but both at Riverside and Laguna Seca Blue Thunder came out on top.

The Jaguars returned to the fray at Charlotte in late May where punctures incurred on the banking cost a number of laps for both cars. Nevertheless, Tullius/Bundy collected second place, Redman/Bedard third, following the demise of Wollek's Mustang and the late retirement of the Holbert/Bell 962, which handed Blue Thunder its third win in a row.

While Group 44 concentrated on Le Mans, Lanier reinforced his points position with second places at Lime Rock and Mid Ohio, behind first the Kreepy Krauly March, then the 962's maiden victory, Bell at the wheel. By the time Group 44 rejoined the series full time at Watkins Glen, Lanier had a total of 105 points to the 47 of Redman and Bundy and the 42 of Tullius. Bedard had been injured in a crash at Indy and had been replaced by twice Le Mans winner and twice IMSA champion Haywood. The Blue Thunder points leader's main title threats were teammate Whittington B. (on 88), Bell (on 65) and Holbert (on 57).

Watkins Glen brought little joy for either Jaguar crew, Redman/Haywood finishing third but a problem-bugged eight laps in arrears of the winning Holbert/Bell 962. Tullius/Bundy retired after separate incidents in each of the two three hour heats.

Back to the west coast, and the Portland race saw victory slip from Tullius' grasp at the eleventh hour .... Car 44 was leading with a mere two laps to run when a rapid fuel stop for a couple of extra gallons let Lanier/Whittington through to win by a frustrating six seconds. Redman/Haywood had another troubled outing, finishing eighth. Nevertheless, Redman and Bundy still had the highest scores of the team and therefore they were entrusted the cars for Sears Point's one hour thrash. Bill Whittington set the pace but Bundy got to within one second

at one stage and Group 44 collected second and third places.

After the sprint race, the Holbert/Bell 962 hit winning form, sweeping to success at Road America and Pocono. With the turbocar up to full speed only fuel economy could give the Jaguar drivers any hope and they were having to push the XJR-5s very hard. Rear suspension and drivetrain problems hurt reliability.

This pattern continued at Michigan and Watkins Glen 2, up to the Daytona finale. In the

meantime, two problem-struck races for Holbert/Bell had confirmed Lanier as the 1984 IMSA Champion.

Daytona's three hour curtain closer saw fuel economy move the Jaguars into the hunt once more, and Bundy was leading after his second stop when he crashed heavily at the chicane, which cost him a top five points table position. Bell/Holbert won but Redman/Haywood finished an encouraging second on the same lap and Redman took sixth in the points standings, the highest placed Group 44 driver with 97 points to the 189 of Lanier.

For 1985 the XJR-5 was significantly revised, with the XJR-7 intended rear end and 10% more power, taking output up to the region of 650 bhp. The revised car proved two seconds a lap quicker around Daytona. On the driver front, Bundy switched to Ford and was replaced by SCCA Formula Super Vee national runner up Chip Robinson. The main opposition to Group 44's two car team was, of course, the 962, with once again the quickest example that of Holbert.

There were six 962s in the 1985 Daytona 24 Hours and the race was Porsche dominated, a challenge from an 725 bhp 3.4 litre Buick V6 turbo driven by John Paul Junior fizzling out in the early stages. The Jaguars qualified some 4½

seconds slower than the quickest 962 but the team was content with its "realistic race times". Indeed, Tullius/Redman/Haywood got well into the hunt, second only to Holbert's car after the first round of fuel stops. The race settled down as a match between these cars and another 962 driven by Bob Wollek and Thierry Boutsen until, at 11 p.m., Tullius had a spectacular crash caused by tyre deflation as he exited the chicane, powering towards the east banking.

Burning pieces of metal and other debris

As in 1983, cars 44 and 14 (left) were major rivals on the IMSA stage. However, this year Holbert's Porsche power propelled a Porsche rather than a March chassis — the 962. This was a long wheelbase version of the 956 campaigned in the World Endurance Championship, the extra inches bringing the pedals back behind the front wheel axis, as per IMSA regulations.

Running in formation at Pocono in 1984 (above): Jaguar's hopes attempt to make up for time lost to the exciting Le Mans bid. Alas, the points deficit was too great to overcome now that the turbo Porsches were up to speed.

was strewn over the track and the alight XJR-5 bodywork began to deform. The cockpit fire extinguisher did its job, but Tullius found he couldn't get the door open and threw off his helmet to put his head through the window, in fear of suffocation. Having torn off his gloves so as to act faster, he suffered minor burns to his hands but thankfully he didn't have to be detained long in hospital.

Car 04, shared by Robinson, Jim Adams and '84 Le Mans team member Claude Ballot-Lena had been an early victim of a blown tyre which had caused body damage and it subsequently retired with zero oil pressure. Miami brought no more cheer for Group 44, Tullius/Robinson's car 44 suffering transmission failure and Redman/Haywood's car 04 hitting the wall and losing a lap it couldn't hope to regain. At Sebring it retired with valve train failure while 44 hit a tyre wall and lost 20 laps, salvaging, as had car 04 at

Miami, fourth place. By the time the Camel trail headed out of Florida the team was understandably down hearted.

At Road Atlanta however, the Jaguars were only two seconds off the turbo pole (Holbert's 962) and after 28 laps, following delays to the quickest Porsche car and John Paul Junior's March-Buick, Redman/Haywood held a secure looking lead. Tullius had meanwhile been hit by a backmarker so hard that his door had popped open, but by the 40 lap mark he had come up to second. John Paul Junior brought his powerful car back to dislodge Tullius/Robinson, only for it to break. The one-two for Jaguar was a tremendous boost for the team and, in California was followed up by a third at Riverside and a second at Laguna Seca for car 44 and a third at Laguna Seca for car 04.

Redman/Haywood backed up their good placings with second places at Charlotte and

Lime Rock on the run up to Le Mans. In fact, Redman had the Lime Rock race in the bag until his windscreen became obscured by oil - so badly that he had to open the door to find the pit road.

By mid '85 the superb handling XJR-5s were the fastest normally aspirated cars in IM-SA, but could do little against Porsches that had been developed to produce around 700 bhp. The Jaguar's main advantage lay in its prodigious torque. This, and Porsche turbo lag, made the Coventry engined car the better package in heavy traffic. Nevertheless, it took all the superb preparation, driving skill, experience and tactical excellence of the ultra-professional Group 44 team to keep the Big Cats so well in the hunt.

As the team prepared to launch its lighter XJR-7 (anticipated as being right down on the

Continuing development of the XJR-5 (left and below) made it the fastest normally aspirated runner in IMSA competition, but gradually the turbocars eased away. Rule changes for 1986 were anticipated in the interests of closer racing.

Jaguar V12 Race Cars

Florida 1985: at Miami car 04 hit a retaining wall and at Sebring car 44 did the same. Note the Corvette styled Lola on the streets of Miami (below) — a hint of General Motors' increasing IMSA involvement. The Porsche 935 evident at Sebring is a throw back to the pre-GTP era. The old warhorse could only hope for success in the 12 and 24 hour races.

Daytona 1985 — Redman keeps 04 ahead of the Kreepy Krauly team's March 84G-Porsche. The race fell to a Porsche 962.

900 kg limit) in August 1985, it was clear that some sort of restriction on the turbo cars would be necessary to keep the normally aspirated runners in with an equal chance of victory. The 725 bhp March-Buick underlined the potential of the turbo car, given unrestricted fuel. IMSA originally set out with 650 bhp 900 kg prototypes in mind and it was clear that some re-thinking was necessary if the blown and unblown runners were once again to enjoy competition on an equal footing.

Despite the uncertainty of the future of the GTP formula, which IMSA was known to be keen to keep as competitive as possible, Dale emphasised the US operation's commitment to prototype racing as a major factor in its marketing strategy, citing racing as "honest, competitive, and a means of providing a manufacturer with an image that cannot be gained as readily in any other way". Against a background of record sales in the USA, he predicted a "golden future" for Group 44, hand-in-hand with the Camel GT Championship.

JAGUAR V12

Return to Le Mans

Le Mans held a special place in Tullius' life as surely as in the history of Jaguar. Tullius first raced in the classic in 1964, as part of the unlucky works Triumph Spitfire team (the cars were crashed by other drivers) and went back in 1968 to drive an intriguing turbine powered Howmet prototype, which fell out of the classification due to a broken hub bearing. As a sports car racing enthusiast, Le Mans has always been his dream, his ultimate goal. It has also been Jaguar's primary target in racing. The marque's desire to build upon its rich Le Mans heritage was a major factor in its acceptance of the prototype project. The XJR-5 was designed specifically as a potential Le Mans car.

Jaguar didn't announce its Le Mans ambitions with the IMSA programme, but Tullius hinted that his contract embraced events outside the USA. In 1983, while Jaguar was increasing its visible motorsport involvement on both sides of the Atlantic, a tentative entry was made for the French 24 Hour race, only to be scratched. That year careful development of the XJR-5 took priority. But following a full season of domestic racing, the XJR-5 and Group 44 were well prepared for a crack at the Big Time.

Jaguar Cars Inc. guided the IMSA project but the Le Mans go ahead, with its worldwide media ramifications, had to be the decision of the parent company. In January of 1984 Coventry said 'lets see how Daytona goes'. It didn't go as

well as it might have, revamped cars suffering too many problems for comfort. However, the promise was still there; the cars were basically strong and were fast - 220 mph on the Daytona banking promised a competitive speed on the Mulsanne straight.

Tullius' worries about how his American team might be received in France were quickly allayed. He told the French press; "the ACO isn't normally very hospitable towards American teams but race director Alain Bertaut reassured me on that point".

Bertaut was one of a number of influential Europeans visiting Daytona. The ACO was indeed keen to attract American entries, and was pressing FISA for a worldwide prototype formula. Soon after Daytona FISA made a sudden announcement to the effect that it would move towards such a concept the following year by bringing its Group C regulations closer to those of GTP.

On the face of it, FISA's proposals looked to be a sell out to IMSA. Firstly it would scrap the proposed tightening of the fuel allowance for the 1984 season and increase the Group C minimum weight to 850 kg, then in 1985 it would abandon the fuel restriction altogether, introducing instead an IMSA-style sliding scale relating engine capacity and type to minimum weight.

Tullius was in favour of a worldwide formula, but FISA's proposals for 1985 did not suit 141

Stretching its legs on the three and a half mile long Mulsanne straight: the appearance of the Big Cat at Le Mans (above) in 1984 brought cheer to every Jaguar enthusiast.

him at all. In FISA's proposed 900 kg class, a 6.0 litre Jaguar would face a Porsche 956 of only slightly reduced, 2500 cc capacity. With no fuel restriction, the Porsche four valve turbo engine could be expected to produce; perhaps 800 bhp?

But neither did Porsche find favour with the proposed formula. It had spent the winter of 1983/84 preparing for a more stringent fuel restriction, and here was FISA putting all that to waste. In the face of such instability the Stuttgart company announced that its works team would boycott Le Mans.

While the arguments raged, Group C was run in 1984 under a continuation of the 1983 fuel allowance (2600 litres for Le Mans) with the higher minimum weight of 850 kg. This increase caused the Porsches and Lancias to have to be

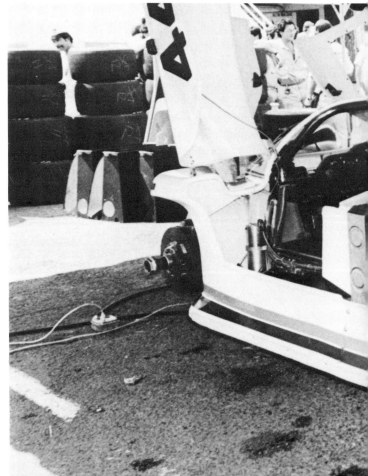

ballasted, lessening the disadvantage of the Jaguar, which tipped the scales to well over 900 kg. From the experience of 1983, it was expected that under the 2600-litre fuel allowance the Porsche and Lancias would race with around 650 bhp, but Jaguar was confident that with the Micos system it would not lag too far behind in the power stakes.

The boycott of Le Mans by the works Porsche team, which had won in impressive style in 1981, '82 and '83, threw the event more open than for many a year. Furthermore, Jaguar felt that its presence at Le Mans might help it get a voice in the discussion about the future of World Championship prototype racing. FISA's proposed IMSA style formula would ironically confine Jaguar to IMSA. Working to the same

end as Porsche, Jaguar's means had to be the opposite.

So the application for entries was once again made. But still it wasn't confirmed. The Miami one-two went some way to dispelling the Daytona doubts, but the final decision by Egan's board would await the outcome of a long distance trial at Pocono in May.

The Pocono exercise meant that Jaguar would have to forfeit a number of IMSA events,

Group 44 was given a prime paddock situation at Le Mans and its ultra-professional turnout was highly impressive to European eyes (below and overleaf).

Jaguar V12 Race Cars

at a time when it held sway at the top of the points standings. Group 44 was serious about its Le Mans intentions.

Claude Ballot-Lena, a former European GT Champion and veteran of 18 Le Mans starts (a record) was confirmed as one of the additional drivers for Le Mans, Tullius, as ever, putting a

A dream come true for Robert Charles Tullius as he and his crew acknowledge the U.S. national anthem, played in honour of their participation in the world's greatest sportscar race. Doc Bundy and Brian Redman are the other drivers visible.

premium on experience. The Frenchman flew to Pocono to make his first acquaintance with the Jaguar on the 2.5 mile tri-oval with its combined tight infield course. Busy circuit schedules meant that the team was only able to secure the venue from 4 pm on 10th May and from 2 pm the following day. A 12-hour run was planned for each session, the entourage catching some sleep in between. On hand, in addition to Ballot-Lena, Tullius, Bundy and the Group 44 crew were Dale and Randle, to represent the decision makers.

A brand new XJR-5 was wheeled out for the trials - so new it lacked the distinctive green stripes. Inevitably there were a few new car

Jaguar leads Porsche at Le Mans in 1984. The radio antenna kept the Group 44 drivers in touch with the pits.

gremlins to be sorted out - a defective starter switch, a mis-set rev limiter and a loose screw, which allowed the grease seal in one front caliper to loosen. But they were straightforward to remedy. The important thing was that the car ran sweetly through its first 12 hours - so sweetly that the test was extended to 15 hours. The only real worry was a herd of deer that was in the habit of grazing on the infield at night. Tullius came upon several on the banking and had to swerve sharply to avoid contact, while Bundy had an even closer avoidance, glancing one unfortunate creature. Thankfully both parties

emerged intact from the moment.

During the night the local police tried to put a stop to the proceedings, arriving at the behest of the local residents. Track officials were able to point out that night use of the circuit was in no way prohibited.

Wheeled out for the pre-race presentations, the smartly prepared Group 44 cars received the biggest cheer at Le Mans in 1984. Media interest was high, the marque's re-appearance giving the race a welcome publicity boost.

Jaguar V12 Race Cars

In line astern, the Jaguar drivers learn the way around the classic French circuit. The instruction was to keep revs down and driving circumspect. To finish first, you must first finish.

After the first stage of the run had been halted at 7.00 am the car was given only routine pitstop maintenance, then the entire crew rested until 2.00 pm. The remaining 9 hours was run off with little bother other than a stripped third gear, allowing Tullius to remark that the test had fulfilled all expectations; "any inadequacies which turned up were easily fixed and were primarily due to using a brand new car".

Randle returned to Browns Lane guardedly
150   optimistic: "with further attention to points of

detail the cars should stand up to the special demands of the 24 Hours at Le Mans. The last three hours were run at considerably higher speed without ill effects. There were some unscheduled stops, but none that would have put the car out of contention in a race...Group 44's cars are well designed and well prepared and the name of Jaguar can only be enhanced by their presence".

A few days later Egan confirmed the entry.

The comeback was made in the light of the realisation that 1984 would be very much a learning year. As Dale said,"it is 27 years since Jaguar last ran its factory team at Le Mans. We don't expect simply to stroll back into the race and duplicate its results. We have a lot to learn and we'll settle this time for having cars that run

well and finish. The development benefits that the Le Mans 24 Hours can give us are what we want".

Soon after the announcement, John Watson was nominated as the team's sixth driver. Britain's out of work Grand Prix driver was contracted to Porsche but was granted special dispensation to switch camps in the light of the boycott, unlike the regular team members. His popular recruitment ensured that there was one British driver in each American car. Watson was teamed with Ballot-Lena and Bedard. Sadly the American was injured in a horrifying barrel-roll at Indianapolis. He was replaced by veteran American road racer Tony 'A to Z' Adamowicz. Like all the team members with the exception of 35 year old Bundy and 37 year old Watson,

Into the night. Car 40 saw dusk at Le Mans 1984, but did not survive until dawn (above). It crashed and ruptured its oil tank, which led to engine seizure. In contrast, car 44 (overleaf) made it through to Sunday morning, before third gear failure heralded a sad retirement for Tullius, Redman and (inset) Bundy.

Adamowicz was in his forties.

Despite the works Porsche boycott, the Le Mans prototype entry was Porsche 956 dominated. Examples of the Bosch Motronic engine management system equipped 2.65 litre, four valve per cylinder turbo engined car were fielded by a number of powerful customer teams, including John Fitzpatrick Racing, Joest Racing, Richard Lloyd Racing, Kremer Racing and Brun Motorsport.

Jaguar V12 Race Cars

Surprisingly, the Porsches weren't the fastest cars in the race. Lancia had developed a 3.0 litre version of its Weber-Marelli management system equipped, four valves per cylinder, Ferrari based turbo engine, and this paid dividends in the race for pole, and in the race itself. Indeed, there was no other team in the race for pole. Lancia Martini put the front row well beyond the reach of the Porsche privateers, turning 3 min. 17.11 sec. to the fastest 956's 3 min. 26.10 sec.

The fastest normally aspirated car was Ray Mallock's heavy (970 kg), flat bottom (Lola T70 based) Aston Martin Downe (neé Nimrod); its 5.3-litre V8 lump churned out 570 bhp and Mallock wrung 3m 33.12s out of the beast, using qualifying tyres.

Jaguar resisted the temptation to chase the works assisted Aston Martin team. Instead, the Group 44 cars were carefully tuned to the circuit, a little extra downforce being found necessary to overcome a tendency to wander on the Mulsanne, this problem not having occurred at Daytona due to the forces generated by running on the banking.

The six drivers concentrated on steady lappery, with strict instructions not to endanger the cars in any way. The rev limit was set at only 6450 rpm. Bundy had a spin at the Ford chicane and wiped the nose off 44, but that was the only

Sunday morning dawns and car 44 is running strongly in the top six (above). A few hours later on the situation will not be so encouraging. The car's untimely retirement served only to increase the team's resolve and the following year the XJR-5s were back once more (right).

untoward incident. Redman clocked 3 min. 35.33 sec. to put 44 on the seventh row, 14th fastest, while Watson clocked 3 min. 39.16 sec. to put 40 on the tenth row after water in the cylinders had necessitated a change of engine and a problem with the Micos system had been rectified.

"With a normally aspirated engine we can't count on the power from a sudden hit of turbo boost. But on the other hand, we can have the sort of times in the race that we had in qualifying", remarked Tullius. He might have added that keeping a car in good shape rather than chasing lap times is what Le Mans has always been about.

As ever immaculately presented, the Big Cats (two race cars plus a brand new spare) were given the rare privilege of a spacious paddock area and were hugely impressive to European eyes. Jaguar's main concern was that not winning would be perceived as failure, whereas the company's target was to finish strongly.

The team commanded huge media attention

Jaguar V12 Race Cars

and got the biggest applause when it wheeled the XJR-5s out to the grid.

Group 44's strategy was to run consistently until Sunday morning, then for one car (40) to charge while (hopefully) many of the turbo cars wilted, the other car continuing to run carefully to the end.

The team's ability to run for longer than the Porsches was evident after the first three-quarters of an hour, when the thirsty 956s started drinking. The Jaguars ran for almost an hour and Tullius had the satisfaction of leading a lap while turbo cars replenished themselves.

As the race settled down into a pattern, the Jaguars were well established in the top ten, running in close company with Mallock's Aston Martin. Tragically, at 9.30 pm Mallock's sister car hit the barrier on the Mulsanne, then his car collided with the wreckage; both AM-Downes were wiped out and a track marshal lost his life in the incident.

The Aston Martin shunt brought out the pace cars for just over an hour, which saved the Porsches a little fuel for some higher boost running later on. The Jaguars continued to hover around sixth and seventh places, on the same lap, until midnight when 'A to Z' brought 40 in with a chunked rear tyre, losing a place.

At 3.00 am, half distance, car 44 was still in the top six and 40 was once again next up in the order. Alas, soon after 4.00 am Ballot-Lena radioed in to report a broken throttle cable. He was instructed to rig up a repair using the spare on board, without falling foul of the regulations by accepting outside assistance. He successfully got the car back to the pits for a proper repair, the entire incident cost eight laps. An hour later there was yet more trouble for 40, this time in the form of a deflating tyre. Adamowicz had no warning of it and flew off the road at Terte Rouge, the right-hander that leads onto the Mulsanne. The car hit the barrier head on, then rebounded, to crunch its left-hand side. The American was able to coax the car back to the pits, unaware that the oil tank in the left flank had been ruptured. The engine was partially seized.

The Tullius/Bundy/Redman car was still

1985 once again saw the American Jaguars sharing the Le Mans limelight with the best from Stuttgart. The XJR-5s (above and right) didn't have the sheer speed to upset the turbocars, but at least car 44 saw the finish. Car 40 (overleaf) once more retired under the cover of night, this year a dud battery stranding it after Adams had striven long and hard to overcome a halfshaft failure.

running strongly as Sunday morning dawned and at 6.00 am still lay in the top six. Alas, soon after 7.00 am, only 25 minutes into Redman's stint, the car came in for an unscheduled stop. Third gear had stripped. It was a repeat of the failure that had occurred during the second phase of the Pocono test, and which had been wrongly diagnosed.

157

During a 24 hour race a car will spend around an hour in the pits even if its run is troublefree, so slow is the permitted refuelling flow rate. In 1985 car 44 spent over three hours in the care of the hard worked Group 44 mechanics, due to an engine management fault followed by a dropped valve. At least some good pit work kept it running to the finish.

It took 46 minutes to repair the gearbox, dropping 44 down to 10th place. By 10.00 am the car was back in the top six, however. Alas, just before 11.30 am Redman felt the gear change stiffen as he approached the Ford chicane before the pits. Unable to get second or third gear, he swept into the pits, where it was

discovered that the gearbox had overheated, probably due to debris from the broken third gear blocking an oil way. With no sure way of removing all the debris, there was the risk of the gearbox seizing before the end of the race - possibly at 200 mph on the Mulsanne. Car 44 was pushed away to a sympathetic ripple of applause.

Encouraged, Jaguar entered four cars for Le Mans in 1985. Two again were to be run by Group 44; the others would be from the TWR World Endurance Championship team. The British outfit had taken delivery of three XJR-5 chassis as an interim measure, to use until such time as its own 850 kgs Group C car would be ready. One of these was fitted with a Coventry developed 48 valve engine: not eligible for GTP

In 1985 Group 44 was honouored to entertain royalty at Le Mans. Here Tullius chats with the Duke of Kent, a great racing enthusiast.

but suitable for Group C - providing it can live with the fuel consumption limitations.

TWR tested the 6.0 litre, four valves/-cylinder engine extensively but, although impressively powerful, it could not be made to live with the 1985 fuel allowance, calling for further development on the engine management system front in particular. The British team resigned itself to race developing its own prototype with two-valve engine power in the WEC, but did not have the 'XJR-6' running until after Le Mans.

The XJR-6 had been designed by Tony Southgate, like Dykstra a well respected free-lancer. Southgate was founder member of the Arrows Grand Prix team, having previously worked on the Lola T70 and a number of Seventies Can Am cars. Once out on his own he had designed the flat bottom Osella Formula One car and the 1983 Ford Group C car, which was still-born due to a change in Ford motorsports policy.

While the Ford was designed around an aluminium honeycomb monocoque, for the XJR-6 Southgate went down the composites route, sandwiching the honeycomb in carbon fibre/Kevlar skins after contemporary Formula One practice to produce a lighter yet stronger structure. The bodywork, rear wing and under-tray are also of composite material.

To keep the wheelbase as short as possible, Southgate's design slots the front of the long V12 engine into a 4½ in. recess in the rear bulkhead and puts the 100 litre bag tank snugly in a wedge-cross section space between that bulkhead and a cockpit moulding which slopes upwards to follow the line of the back of the driver's seat. The V12 is carried as a fully stressed member and is mated to a March/Hewland five-speed gearbox designed specifically to cope with the torque of a 750 bhp turbo engine. Its radiator is carried horizontally in the nose, air entering through a long narrow opening, the bottom edge of which is formed by the front splitter. At the other end of the car is a full width wing but this is little more than a trim tab for the XJR-6 is a ground effect car, its over and under body shapes designed with reference to the Imperial College, London wind tunnel.

Jaguar V12 Race Cars

Southgate neatly tucked the rear spring/-damper units into 19 in. wheel rims to allow maximum width for the ground effect producing venturi tunnels. These units are hung vertically from a transverse cross-member which is supported by the gearbox. With the upper wishbone and the cross-member above the tunnels, only the lower wishbone and driveshaft pass through the venturis.

At the front the spring/damper units are mounted almost horizontally above the driver's feet and are pushrod operated. Like the 1985 works Porsche 962Cs, the XJR-6 runs Dunlop boltless 'Denloc' tyres on big diameter rims, 17 in. at the front.

The first the XJR-6 came out at around 865 kg and started testing in July. Subsequent race cars were expected to be right down on the weight limit and were scheduled to début in August/September to allow plenty of development prior to Le Mans 1986. Group 44 planned a similar programme for its composite monocoque XJR-7, elements of which were incorporated in the revised 1985 XJR-5, as recounted in the last chapter. This car warmed up encouragingly for the 1985 French Classic with "qualifying times and a finishing record satisfactory for the run up to Le Mans", as Tullius put it.

This year the aim was to contest the French race without interrupting the IMSA schedule, and the team was even able to run a single car at Mid Ohio, just two days before scrutineering took place in France.

After Porsche's 1984 boycott, the FISA had relented on its proposed IMSA style formula and had introduced the tighter fuel restriction, albeit a year late. For 1985 the limit was 2100 litres at Le Mans, which could be expected to slow the Porsches. Even the ever-victorious works cars - the favourites. Early season 1000 km races had seen the turbocars racing with closer to 600 than 650 bhp.

Tullius made it clear that his 1985 objective was to win. Alas, the V12 engine was surprisingly hard hit by the reduced fuel allocation. In practice the Big Cats ran 7500 rpm and lapped 2.5 seconds faster than in 1984, the revised XJR-5 chassis so stable Redman reported that he could take the notorious Mulsanne kink on either side of the road. But then a detonation problem occurred.

The team had taken both cars over full of fuel (hence the 80 kg overweight scrutineering weights of around 1000 kg) and didn't experience any problem until after the cars had been refuelled during the break in Wednesday's practice: both engines were lost Wednesday night.

Detonation can be caused by either timing, compression ratio or fuel quality. The team had no control over fuel quality as the organisers provide a compulsory supply and it wasn't feasible to alter the compression ratio so the timing was backed off - to the detriment of fuel economy. Although the fuel quality appeared to improve during the meeting the team didn't dare run timing higher again - it only had four engines ....

Tullius was looking for another strong first hour showing but a vibration problem (which turned out to be an out of balance wheel) put paid to that.

Normally revs creep up during a long race as the engine loosens but Group 44 kept its cars under 7000 rpm and a combination of driving technique and leaning off of the engine helped reduce consumption from an initial 4.2 miles per gallon to 4.6. Neither car featured in the midnight top ten. Just after half distance car 40 (Redman/Haywood/Jim Adams) coasted to a halt

Car 44 at Le Mans (previous page) in 1984 and (inset) 1985; only detail differences such as the location of the towing hook, type of wing mirror, and so forth, are evident.

Will she make it? Tullius (right) waits patiently while his crew attends to the dropped valve that came so close to costing him a finish at Le Mans in 1985.

The TWR XJR-6 on a pre-race test run at Snetterton in Norfolk. The carbon composite monocoque car was tested extensively in the summer of '85 prior to its Mosport World Endurance Championship race debut in mid August.

just past the pits with a broken cv joint. The resourceful Adams isolated the axle, but having parked in a dangerous position he had been advised to keep the car's lights on. The battery would not then restart the car.

Car 44 (Tullius/Robinson/Ballot-Lena) running steadily but still outside the top ten, struck

a misfire problem on Sunday morning and lost a total of 40 minutes through changes of Micos electronics. The problem was that there was a spot where the throttle pedal sensor wasn't making contact. The first replacement sensor had the same problem ...

With 90 minutes still to run and now, thanks to general attrition, at least a top ten placing in sight, the car dropped a valve. A valve spring retainer had broken: the valve fell in and a small portion of it was actually punched clean through the cylinder head.

It was a very tricky job to seal off the cylinder — the camshaft had to be broken with a hammer and chisel, to de-activate the valves.

Then the cylinder had to be filled through the plug hole with liquid rubber which, after 15 minutes setting time, held the debris in place it wasn't possible to clean out the cylinder in the time available. Finally, the injection system was disconnected and, of course, the plug was left out. The car ran so well on 11 cylinders that Tullius drove the lap a little too quickly and had to complete 17 miles before he was able to see the finish, and collect a 13th place classification.

"This is an event that takes experience. We're gaining that rapidly. Next year we will be more competitive", summarized the ever-determined Tullius, delighted at least to have experienced what must be the world's most satisfying finish.

JAGUAR V12

Specifications

GROUP 44 E TYPE

SCCA B Production 1974/5

Modified Series 3 E-type roadster rolling chassis.
Steel body panels. GRP front air dam.
Jaguar 4-speed gearbox
Jaguar cast-iron brake discs - outboard front,
inboard rear.
Twin calipers - AP four pot.
Minolite rims - front and rear 8½ in. x 15 in.
Single front located Harrison water radiator.
Single front located Serck oil radiator.
14-gallon fuel tank in boot. 4-gallon oil tank in
passenger footwell.
Wheelbase 105 in.; front track 56 in.; rear track
56 in.
Dry weight 2670 lb.
Ferodo pads, Koni dampers, AP clutch,
Goodyear tyres.
Wet or dry sump engine - standard carburation.
Max. bhp: 460. Max. rpm: 7000/7500.

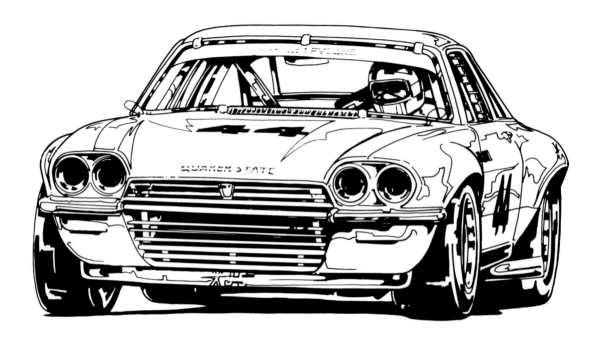

GROUP 44 XJ-S

SCCA Trans Am Category 1 1976

Modified XJ-S coupé rolling chassis.
Steel body panels. GRP bonnet and front air dam.
Jaguar 4-speed gearbox.
AP cast-iron brake discs - outboard front, inboard rear.
Twin calipers - AP four pot.
Minolite, later Jongbloed rims - front and rear 10 in. x 15 in.
Single front located Hurst water radiator.
Twin front located Serck oil radiators.
32-gallon fuel tank in boot. 5-gallon oil tank in boot.
Wheelbase 102 in.; front track 61 in.; rear track 60 in..
Dry weight 3150 lb.
Ferodo pads, Koni dampers, AP clutch, Goodyear tyres.
Dry sump engine - 6 Weber carburettors.
Max. bhp: 525. Max rpm: 7500/8000.

GROUP 44 XJ-S

SCCA Trans Am 1981

Group 44 steel tube spaceframe with modified
XJ-S suspension.
Steel roof, aluminium doors, bonnet and boot.
GRP fenders and front and rear spoilers.
Jaguar 4 or 5-speed gearbox.
AP cast iron brake discs - outboard front,
inboard rear.
Single calipers - AP four pot.
Jongbloed rims - front and rear 10 in. x 15 in.
Single front located Harrison water radiator.
Twin front located Airesearch oil radiators.
27-gallon fuel tank in boot. 5-gallon oil tank in
boot.
Wheelbase 102 in.; front track 62 in.; rear track
60 in.
Dry weight 2560 lb.
AP pads, Koni dampers, AP clutch, Goodyear
tyres.
Dry sump engine - 6 Weber carburettors.
Max. bhp: 570. Max. rpm: 8000.

BROADSPEED XJ12C

Group 2 1976/7

Modified XJ12C coupé rolling chassis.
Steel body panels. GRP arch extensions and
spoilers.
Jaguar 4-speed gearbox.
AP cast-iron brake discs - outboard front,
inboard rear.
Single rear calipers, twin front - AP four pot.
BBS or Ronal rims - front 12 in. rear
14 in. x 16 in. dia.
Single front located Serck water radiator.
Single front located Serck oil radiator.
27-gallon fuel tank in boot. 2-gallon oil tank in
boot.
Wheelbase 113 in.; front and rear track 58 in..
Dry weight 3197 lb.
AP pads, Armstrong dampers, AP clutch,
Dunlop tyres.
Wet sump engine - Lucas fuel injection.
Max. bhp: 560. Max rpm: 8000.

TWR XJ-S

Group A 1982/4

Modified XJ-S coupé rolling chassis.
Steel body panels. GRP front spoiler.
Getrag 5-speed gearbox.
AP cast-iron brake discs - outboard front and
rear.
Single calipers - AP four pot.
Speedline rims - front 11 in. rear
11.5 in. x 17 in. dia.
Single front located Serck water radiator.
Single front located Serck oil radiator.
27-gallon fuel tank in boot.
Wheelbase 102 in.; front track 59 in.; rear track
58 in.
Dry weight 3086 lb.
Ferodo pads, Bilstein dampers, AP clutch,
Dunlop tyres.
Wet sump engine - TWR fuel injection.
Max. bhp: 450. Max. rpm: 7300.

GROUP 44 XJR-5

IMSA GTP 1982/5

Group 44 aluminium monocoque prototype chassis.
Kevlar and carbon fibre body panels. Ground effect underbody.
Rear wing.
Hewland 5-speed gearbox.
AP cast-iron brake discs - outboard front and rear.
Single calipers - AP four pot.
Jongbloed rims - front 12 in. rear 14 in. x 15 in. dia.
Later BBS 16 in. dia.
Twin side located Alan Docking water radiators.
Single side located Setraub oil radiator.
27-gallon fuel tank in mid position. 4-gallon oil tank in left side pod.
Wheelbase 108 in.front track 66 in.; rear track 62 in.
Dry weight 1900 lb.

AP pads, Koni dampers, AP clutch, Goodyear tyres.
Dry sump engine - 6 Weber carburettors. Later Lucas-Micos engine management system.
Max. bhp: 610-670. Max. rpm: 8100.

TWR XJR-6

Group C 1985

TWR carbon fibre/Kevlar monocoque prototype chassis

Carbon fibre/Kevlar body panels. Ground effect underbody.

Rear wing.

March 5-speed gearbox

AP cast iron brake discs - outboard front and rear.

Single calipers - AP four pot.

Speedline rims - front 12 in. x 17 in. dia., rear 15 in. x 19 in. dia.

Single front located Serck water radiator

Twin side located Serck oil radiators.

100-litre fuel tank in mid position.

12-litre oil tank in front left-hand side of engine bay.

Wheelbase 2780 mm; front track 1500 mm; rear track 1500 mm

Dry weight 870 kg

Ferodo pads, Koni dampers, AP clutch, Dunlop tyres.

Dry sump engine - Lucas Micos engine management system

Max bhp: 640. Max rpm: 8000